The

TREE

in my

GAR
DEN

The
TREE
in my
GAR

Choose one tree, plant it — and change the world

DEN

KATE BRADBURY

Illustrated by **LUCILLE CLERC**

Contents

Why trees?
Why now?

Our world is on fire. Literally, in parts of California, Europe and Australia, wildfires are tearing through forests and communities, killing people and wildlife. Metaphorically, too, parts of the world burn so hot we will soon be unable to live in them. But, rather than feeling hopeless, let's join together to plant trees. Starting in our gardens.

Climate change and its associated effects of biodiversity loss and extreme weather events make for grim reading. The sixth assessment report from the Intergovernmental Panel on Climate Change, written in 2022, warns that time is running out to act to avoid catastrophe. Temperatures are rising, rivers are flooding or drying up, species are dying out. In 2021, more than 400 weather stations broke their heat records, with the highest temperatures in Canada increasing by a whopping 4.6 per cent, to 49.6°C (121.3°F), and the Pakistan city of Jacobabad logging temperatures of 52°C (126°F). There, the heat and extreme humidity have been deemed too much for the human body to bear.

We're staring down the barrel of mechanical pollination because there are no longer insects to do the job for us; of cloud seeding technologies to make it rain because rain doesn't fall where we need it to; of not being able to live in vast swathes of Earth due to extremes of heat, humidity, flooding and wind.

How did we get here?
Well, it all started with deforestation. In the last 6,000 years we have lost half of our forests in Europe, as space has been taken for agriculture and growing human populations. Deforestation continues today, mostly in tropical regions such as Brazil, where global demand for cheap beef drives competition for land. And now, for the first time, the Amazon rainforest is thought to emit more carbon dioxide than it can absorb due to deforestation and changing weather patterns. Around the world,

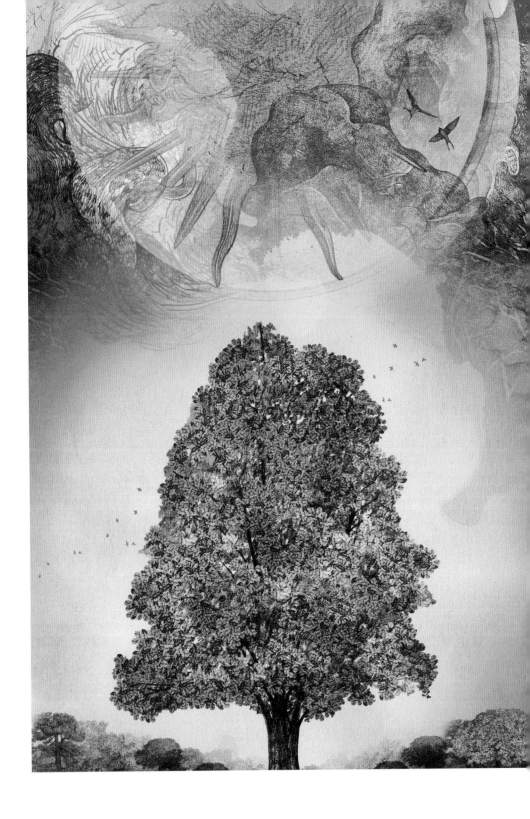

we destroy around 10 million hectares (25 million acres) of forest every year, which adds up to an area about the size of Portugal each decade.

It's not just deforestation that causes climate change. Use of fossil fuels – from cars and planes to space rockets – the intensification of agriculture, particularly the global meat and fish industries, and the consumption of peat, along with the mismanagement of peat bogs and moorland, all play their part.

And yet there is hope.

What can we do next?
Some 50 per cent of deforestation in the world is offset by regrowing or new forests, which should only increase as global awareness of climate change and deforestation expands. More of us are buying less and recycling more, taking fewer flights and eating less meat. But – and I'm not going to beat around the bush here (pardon the pun) – we're in a difficult situation. We can get out of it, at least in part, and depending on how quickly we act, with the help of the things we chopped down in the first place: trees! You could plant one in your garden today.

Trees are only part of the solution to tackling climate change and loss of biodiversity. We need to change the way we treat the world's oceans, our remaining peat bogs, grasslands and ponds. Carbon is stored in a wide range of habitats, including our gardens, and we need to protect them all. We can (and should) join environmental organisations and wildlife charities, sign petitions and make better choices when food shopping and at polling stations.

But there's something about tree planting that gives us ownership of the issue, that rewards us for, and reminds us of, what we've done. We plant a tree, water it and watch it grow. We marvel at birds landing in its branches, at insects eating its leaves and pollinating its flowers. We might eat its fruit and share it with the wildlife, and fall in love with its glorious autumn colouring. We might sit beneath it and listen to the rustle of its leaves, or put our ear to its trunk to hear the gurgle of rising sap in spring.

Trees are great. They root us to the land and connect us to the seasons. People tell me "it's not spring until my hawthorn flowers" and "not summer until I've eaten my first cherry". At Christmas we bring trees into our homes and make wreaths with berry-laden branches.

For me, the turning of the seasons is marked by the achingly long days of waiting for the first leaves to unfurl on my garden trees after winter (I have three: a rowan, hawthorn and silver birch; pp.14–15).

In planting, and observing, trees, we notice more and are more mindful as a result. Our blood pressure lowers, our mental health improves. On top of that, trees breathe in carbon dioxide and breathe out oxygen, they help support insect, mammal and bird populations, prevent flooding, stabilise temperatures and filter wind. Trees are amazing, aren't they? To think we ever chopped them down. To think we're still chopping them down!

Plant a tree

As the old Chinese proverb goes, "The best time to plant a tree was 20 years ago. The second best time is now". By planting a tree you will directly help to reduce some of the effects of climate change. Each drop of water absorbed by the tree's roots is a drop that won't join others to form a puddle, a flood. Each milligram of carbon dioxide taken in by its leaves will reduce the amount floating in the atmosphere. Each bee that visits its flowers will not go hungry, each egg laid on its leaves will provide food for species further up the food chain.

To plant a tree is to give life – to wildlife, to you, to your children and grandchildren. Planting trees is an act of power and rebellion, a big two fingers up to a world of greed and corruption. As you lower your tree's roots into the ground and cover them with soil, you become part of a global reforestation movement. Isn't that something?

Trees are amazing. To think we ever chopped them down. To think we're still chopping them down!

Why gardens?

It's estimated that there are around 27 million households in the UK, and just over 22 million of us have a garden. If every one of us planted a tree in our gardens tomorrow, that would be 22 million more trees in the UK, each one absorbing carbon dioxide while providing food and homes for wildlife, not to mention giving us something nice to look at. 22 million trees. Tomorrow.

How much nectar and pollen would 22 million trees add for our beleaguered bees? How many more leaves would there be for moths to lay their eggs on and caterpillars to eat? How many more baby birds would have bellies full of those caterpillars, plus the aphids, leaf miners and other bugs that also eat leaves and live among trees? How many more hedgehogs would be able to gather fallen leaves from beneath these trees, to line their cosy dens in autumn?

Trees are life
Each one is a city, home to hundreds of beings, from the tiniest thrips to the wriggliest caterpillars and the largest birds. In planting one we might create some much-needed shade in the garden, a focal point, maybe, somewhere to sit under as our feet poke out into the sun. But, in doing so, we create something so much more wonderful. We provide somewhere for a bird to land as it checks out our feeders or bird box. We provide a trunk for a squirrel to shimmy up, in hot pursuit of another squirrel, in spring. We provide flowers for bees, leaves for caterpillars, berries for birds. We provide little nooks and crannies in the bark where a queen wasp might take shelter over winter. We provide a view through a window, from which we might marvel at spring blossom, autumn leaf colour or nesting birds. Something that connects us to the outside, no matter what time of year it is, through which we can measure the passing of time.

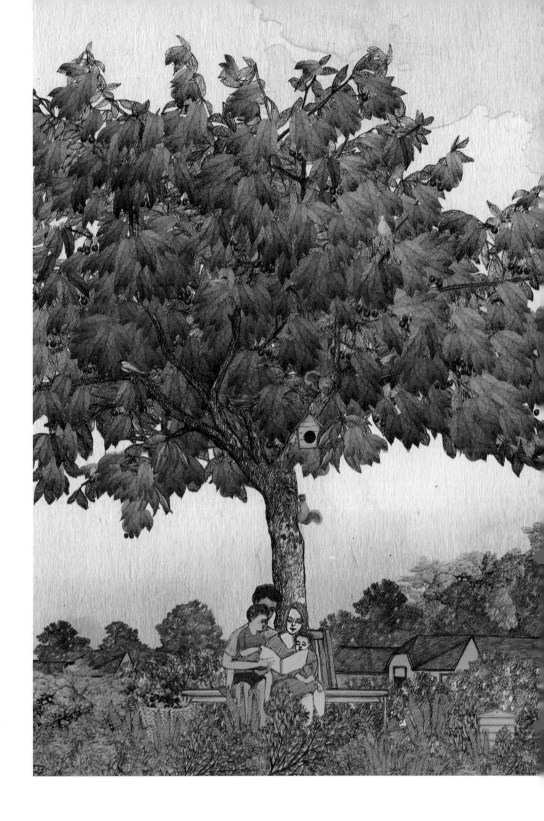

And, as each day passes, as each bird lands on a branch and each caterpillar munches a leaf, that tree in your garden is absorbing carbon dioxide. One tree, in one garden. It probably won't make much difference, will it? But 22 million trees? Why, that's a forest.

Creating a network

Combined, our 22 million gardens have the potential to become a wildlife reserve in their own right. Knitted together via holes in or beneath fences and gates, they comprise a network of habitats the length and breadth of the country. Gardens mimic habitats we call the "woodland edge", where shrubs and small trees grow among grasses and wildflowers. The wildlife we attract to our gardens reflects that – the birds, amphibians, bees and butterflies that visit are all creatures of the woodland edge. So our gardens are pre-destined for tree planting – trees belong in our gardens, no matter how big or small they are.

You might see the space outside your front or back door as small and meaningless, but with a few choice plants it can act as a stepping stone from one habitat to the next. What's a stepping stone, you ask? Imagine a long, grey road bookended by green spaces, with the wildlife in each space cut off from the other because the long grey road between them is too long and too grey – there's no shelter or food to help them on their journey. Add a few gardens and suddenly the wildlife can move – bees and butterflies can drink nectar to give them energy to fly, frogs and hedgehogs can hide beneath a hedge or shrub. These stepping-stone habitats are crucial in the fight against climate change and biodiversity loss because they allow wildlife to move around – that is, they connect habitats, enabling wildlife to find more suitable habitats if they need to. Studies have shown that some insect species are already moving north, in search of cooler temperatures. If there are too many long, grey roads on their journey they're not going to survive.

Choosing the right tree

The space outside your front or back door, then, has the potential to save lives and promote biodiversity. You just need to plant it up. Tree planting can seem daunting at first. You may be anxious about your tree growing too big, casting too much shade or shedding too many leaves. And what will the neighbours say if you reduce the light to their garden? These are all valid points, which is why it's vital to take your time when choosing the tree in your garden (see pp.52–143). The right tree will bring you years of enjoyment, wildlife watching and a feeling of having done something "good". The wrong tree will lead to years of anxiety after which you, or someone else who inherits the space, will have to chop it down.

Before you plant your tree, think about what you want from it. How tall will it grow in your lifetime? How wide or dense will its canopy be? If you need privacy you could plant a tree with a dense canopy, such as an ornamental pear, or if you prefer filtered light then go for something like a silver birch, with its airy canopy, thin branches and small leaves. For the best wildlife options, it's a good idea to choose native trees (see

pp.20–21) as these have evolved with the species you want to protect. To take account of climate change you might consider a tree from a more southerly region, as global heating could mean it survives better in 50 years' time. Do you want fruit or berries (see pp.40–41)? Autumn colour (see pp.42-43) or year-round interest? Some trees really have it all.

This book offers information about a lot of trees, which you can compare and contrast before making your big planting decision. You'll also find lots of reasons why you should plant trees, because I want to hammer home how important and joyful they are. I hope, in reading this book, you will be armed with all the knowledge you need to plant and care for your garden tree. I also hope we can reforest the British Isles, one garden at a time.

One tree, in one garden. It probably won't make much difference, will it? But 22 million trees? Why, that's a forest.

The trees in my garden

I moved into my house in January 2019. A Victorian terrace, it has a narrow, 12m (40ft) garden that backs on to other houses and, beyond it, a park. I had high hopes for lots of wildlife. But the garden was planted with things that held little value for them: a huge Japanese spindle, a common jasmine, a eucalyptus tree that was planted far too close to the house. I set to work immediately.

Wishing to start from a blank canvas, I dug up everything. I kept what was useful and donated the rest to friends and neighbours. And then I started again from scratch.

My trees

I planted the trees first: a gorgeous rowan (*Sorbus aucuparia*), a Midland hawthorn (*Crataegus laevigata*) and a silver birch (*Betula pendula*). They instantly gave shape to the garden and provided me with a window into a world I hadn't finished creating. I planted them when they were dormant and I still remember my excitement as the first leaf buds burst in spring – the freshest green on twigs that had been bare for so long.

What followed has been endlessly delightful. I marvelled at the first birds that landed in the trees as they navigated around the newly designed space. I listened and watched as the first bees found the first flowers, laughed as the first blackbirds found the first berries. Imagine my joy when I kicked my first pile of fallen leaves. I fell in love with my trees as soon as I planted them, and my love for them grows as well as they do.

Rowan

At the back of the garden is the rowan. I chose it because it won't grow too big and it has gorgeous flat plates of spring blossom, followed by fat red berries. I love watching its mitten-like buds form in late winter, and burst into beautiful pinnate leaves. Many pollinators use its flowers, while blackbirds and robins eat its berries. Other species visit for shelter – everything from squirrels to starlings.

Hawthorn

Three metres (10ft) from the rowan is the hawthorn, a slightly smaller tree that shouldn't outgrow the garden. The space between them is enough for their roots to exchange food and information, and one day I hope their canopies will meet, too. It has single white blossoms loved by bees, then dark red "haws" that birds rely upon in autumn. Its leaves are popular with many moths, which I hope will use the tree for breeding when it's more mature. Its twiggy frame will make the perfect spot for birds to nest, too.

Silver birch

On the other side is the silver birch, the tallest tree in the garden, but the shortest-lived. I love its heart-shaped leaves that have been found by leaf miners and buff-tip caterpillars, and its beautiful, peeling bark. I planted it because I wanted to watch blue tits hang upside down from its slender branches and pick at its catkins. Watching them do this fills my heart on even the darkest winter days. In November, it's the most gorgeous thing for miles; its leaves turn yellow, before falling into a satisfying pile.

Making room for more trees

If I had a bigger garden I'd plant more: I'd have my own arboretum if I could. Instead I make do with smaller specimens: a tiny mixed hedge of hawthorn, hazel, field rose and common buckthorn. Then there are two much smaller trees: a Kilmarnock willow and a strawberry tree. The willow is at its maximum height and sits at the edge of my pond, and the strawberry tree is in a pot, in which it will grow some more before I find space for it in the garden.

I love watching the rowan's mitten-like buds form in late winter, and burst into beautiful pinnate leaves.

UNDERSTANDING TREES

Having evolved over millennia, trees are the foundations for so much life on Earth. It's easy to say that we need to plant more trees, but if we want to make a more meaningful difference, knowing which varieties to plant – and where – is crucial. By getting to know trees before you plant, you'll be able to reap more rewards later on.

Trees over time

Trees have been growing on Earth for around 400 million years. Some of the earliest species can still be seen in gardens today, including the monkey puzzle tree (Araucaria araucana), and the maidenhair tree (Ginkgo biloba); they evolved around 248 million years ago, which is why they're sometimes known as living fossils.

Over the millennia, the shape of trees, the way they absorb water and nutrients, and how they reproduce, have all evolved to ensure trees are as successful as they can be in their given environment. Each tree's leaf shape, bark, flowers, fruit and seeds are the way they are for very specific reasons.

Trees have adapted to grow in wet or dry soils, up mountains or in valleys, in rainforests and cloud forests – every environment has a set of perfectly adapted trees that grow successfully in it. Most trees thrive in a community growing alongside others, but some do best growing on their own. The black walnut tree, for example, secretes a chemical called juglone from its roots, which can inhibit the growth of nearby plants.

Tree shape

Trees have evolved their shape to make the most of available light levels. The crown of broadleaf trees (such as oak) is large and rounded so their leaves can absorb light in cloudy, temperate environments. Conifers, typically from colder climates, tend to be cone-shaped as this helps them absorb light when the sun is low on the horizon (resulting in weaker rays). Cone-shaped trees are also able to shed snow easily.

Leaf shape and size

Leaf shape is determined by the need to absorb light and carbon dioxide, but other factors such as climate, temperature, day length, water availability, nutrition and predators influence shape, too. Large leaves absorb more light than smaller ones,

UNDERSTANDING TREES

but lose moisture via evaporation, and can scorch in too much sun. Evergreen trees have leaves that are shaped to minimise evaporation. To prevent water loss, leaves may be tiny, needle-like, waxy, glossy, lobed or toothed.

Protection from predators

The outer bark protects a tree from disease and damage – many species, including oaks and willows, have bark containing tannins unpalatable to mammals. The bark helps the tree to retain moisture and protects living cells from infections from bacteria, fungi and other pathogens. Some trees also grow thorns to protect leaves and seeds from being eaten.

Flowers, fruit, nuts and seeds

Each stage of a tree's reproductive cycle has evolved to suit its local climate and pollinating wildlife. Tree flowers have evolved to be pollinated by wind or insects (see pp.40–41) in order to produce fruit. Most fruits have evolved to be eaten by birds or mammals, which then pass the seeds of the fruit through their digestive system, and disperse them elsewhere. Winged seeds such as those of sycamore are carried on the wind. Other trees have evolved more interesting ways to reproduce. The crack willow is so called because of the loud cracking noise its branches make when they fall off the tree and into water below, in which they are carried downstream, sometimes rooting into a new area of riverbank.

Trees today

Today, trees still grow in their native environments (see pp.20–21), but human intervention has also seen them growing in locations you wouldn't otherwise find them. Victorian plant hunters paved the way for trees to be grown in regions far from their origins, bringing back seeds of trees such as Chinese magnolia, and giant redwood from California. Most of the ornamental trees we grow in our gardens today are not native: Himalayan birch, Japanese maple, Canadian redbud, Australian eucalyptus and Turkey oak are examples that all hail from regions beyond our own.

What's more, plant breeders have crossed closely related trees to create hybrids. These trees may be crossed to improve resistance to disease, grow taller or shorter, have a more ornamental growth habit, such as weeping branches, or bear more flowers or fruit.

Native or non-native?

A native tree is generally considered to be one that has grown in a given place since the last Ice Age, and is therefore perfectly adapted to the climate it lives in. But today's climate is changing too quickly for many trees to evolve and adapt in time to the new conditions – should we therefore be looking to non-natives to grow in their place?

In the UK, trees colonised the land after the glaciers melted, some 11,500 years ago, when Britain was still connected to mainland Europe. As such, they have evolved closely with the wildlife that have also colonised the land after the ice retreated. Native trees and other plants are therefore better for wildlife than non-natives. Simply put, they already have relationships in place: they flower when pollinators need flowers and bear berries and seeds when birds need those berries and seeds. Moths lay eggs on the leaves of (often specific) native trees, at exactly the right time for their caterpillars to be the perfect size for baby birds to digest. Native trees, plants and their corresponding wildlife grow together as part of a series of complex ecosystems that have evolved over the last 11,500 years – and as a wildlife gardener I cram as many native species into my garden as possible.

But native trees are struggling. Research has shown that many British natives such as beech and oak are already suffering stresses from drought, which is putting pressure on their ability to flower and fruit (which has a knock-on effect on wildlife). This is on top of the numbers of pests and diseases that are now surviving here thanks to warmer conditions. If trees weren't suffering from drought, would they be able to better deal with some of the many other problems they now face?

Matching trees with climate

Climate scientists at Gothenburg University predict that the current climate of southeast Europe is close to what we can expect in the UK in 30–50 years' time: ultimately warmer and drier. With that in mind, should we be planting trees from the Balkans, which are better able to cope with hotter, drier summers, rather than native species? Balkan natives include the lilac and the horse chestnut. Trees from China, Mexico and North America could also be better suited to growing in our drier climate in future.

And what about palm trees? While they store far less carbon than deciduous trees, many have evolved to grow in hot, dry, coastal conditions, and are especially adapted to growing in high winds. Could they have a role in our gardens?

As well as planting trees from warmer, drier regions, we can also look at growing ranges. Many of our native trees, including English oak and beech, grow across Europe, into the Caucasus, where rainfall is much lower. While some of these trees in the Caucasus may be a separate subspecies to those growing in the UK, they are essentially native, and using seeds from them could help future-proof our forests.

Human-made hybrids could also work, where closely related trees are crossed to introduce natural resilience to both climate change and diseases. This technique has worked before: *Ulmus* 'New Horizon' is a hybrid of Japanese and Siberian elms. It's completely resistant to Dutch Elm disease, introduced to Britain from Canada in the 1960s, which wiped out most of our elms. Being so closely related to our native elms, could the wildlife that use elms, such as the white letter hairstreak butterfly, be tempted by these new hybrids, and so have a better chance of survival?

The way forward

It seems to me that the most sensible route in British gardens is to plant a mix of natives and carefully selected non-natives. We need native trees now for our native wildlife now. Planting more British trees will create corridors through which British wildlife can travel, especially as they will need to move north as temperatures increase. But we also need to plant trees now that will cope better with the increased temperatures and humidity of the future. And that's where non-natives come in. But we must choose non-natives that support biodiversity, to enable better adaptations to our changing climate and, ultimately, more survival.

Trees and fungi

Fungi get a bad press in gardens, which is sad, because they mostly do a lot of good. Fungi are essential for the growth and health of garden trees. The mushrooms or toadstools we see above the soil's surface are the fruiting bodies, a tiny part of the main body of the fungus, whose string-like fungal threads (hyphae) live below the surface, on or around tree roots in networks known as mycelium.

Many trees depend on fungi to help them grow. In woodlands, miles of hyphae grow underground, connecting tree roots to the soil and enabling them to better take up water and nutrients. These mycorrhizal (fungus–root) partnerships also link the root systems of different trees to each other, creating networks of trees sometimes referred to as the "wood wide web". In some species, such as beech, fungi enable trees to support each other, with healthy trees giving nutrients to less healthy ones. The more we learn about trees the more we realise they are a community species. So that one tree in your garden could well be connected to the tree next door, through a fungal network, with which they exchange nutrients, carbon and information. In return, the tree provides the fungi with sugars – unlike plants, fungi do not photosynthesise, so rely on other living bodies to provide them with the energy they need.

Some fungi can protect trees from drought, disease and predators. Gardeners are forever trying to get rid of fairy rings on lawns, despite the fact that the *Marasmius oreades* fungus responsible feeds the lawn and improves its health. Honey fungus is known only for its tree-and shrub-killing properties, but there are several species, some co-existing with trees and shrubs for years. In soils contaminated with heavy metals, fungi can help to remove them.

Fungi are amazing, and deserve more recognition. Different fungi have different specialisms, so the greater variety of fungi available to your tree, the healthier it will be.

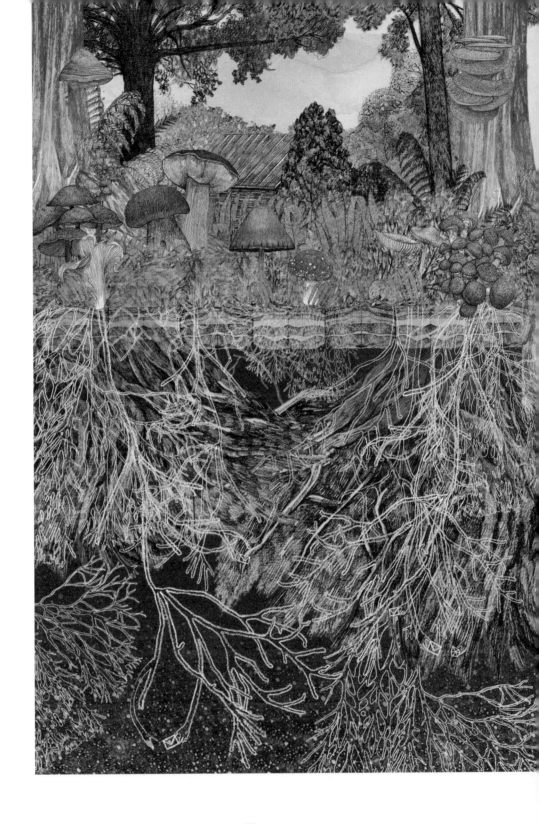

To plant or not to plant?

As trees grow, they pull in carbon dioxide via their leaves (see p.34), and store it in their trunk, roots and branches. When they die, that carbon is released slowly back into the atmosphere. Planting trees can, therefore, help slow climate change, as the more trees we plant the more carbon dioxide is absorbed. But trees alone will not solve climate change, and tree planting can sometimes do more harm than good.

In Britain, millions of trees have been planted in recent years, and this is continuing in gardens, towns and in rural areas. Elsewhere, trees are being planted with even more gusto: the Indian state of Uttar Pradesh claims to have planted 50 million trees in one day. The Great Green Wall of the Sahara and the Sahel is an ambitious international project, which involves the planting of trees across the Sahel to prevent the expansion – or desertification – of the Sahara Desert . If you're looking for a good news story, look no further than Costa Rica, which doubled its forest cover in just 30 years.

As citizens of tree-poor countries, we're encouraged to plant trees to help fight climate change, but it's worth pausing for breath before we reach for the spade.

When not to plant trees

The first thing to consider is that not all land was originally forested. As well as woodland, in the British Isles there are grasslands, wetlands and peat bogs – landscapes where trees don't belong. These complex habitats store carbon in their own right – it's estimated that the world's peat bogs store twice as much carbon as its forests. Grasslands store less carbon than woodlands but the storage is more reliable – grasslands are less at risk from forest fires, for example, which can quickly release thousands of tonnes of carbon back into the atmosphere. The carbon storage of our 22 million gardens, with their accumulated plants, trees, lawns and ponds, shouldn't be sniffed at, either.

It goes without saying that, rather than replanting forests, we should be protecting those we already have, from ancient woodland felled in the UK for projects such as HS2 and roadbuilding, to the Amazon rainforest lost to cattle ranches in Brazil. Protecting existing woodland is much better for preventing climate change and supporting wildlife than planting new trees, which take time to sequester (store) carbon and offer the habitats of established forests.

Natural regeneration

Another alternative is to let land revert to its original state, with minimum input from us humans. Termed "rewilding", this system could be used instead of mass planting schemes. A study published in 2021 suggests that half of Britain's new forests have been planted not by humans, but by jays, which bury acorns in autumn. Along with grey squirrels, jays bury acorns to eat later when food runs low, but often forget about them – and a woodland is born.

Letting wildlife replant our forests will have many benefits: no plastic tree guards littering the landscape, no need to water vulnerable saplings, no digging of the soil (which in itself releases carbon). Animals are brought in to "manage" the habitat: highland cows and pigs, which graze the land gently, allow some species to grow while preventing total reforestation.

Rewilding isn't appropriate for gardens or for our cities and parks, so in these habitats we must plant trees. But let's do so armed with the knowledge that trees like to grow together, that scrub is an invaluable wildlife habitat, and that, on its own, your one tree is simply not enough to reverse, or even slow down the effects of climate change.

Half of Britain's new forests are thought to have been planted by jays, which bury acorns in autumn.

Trees in cities

We already know that trees absorb carbon dioxide, improve wellbeing and provide homes for wildlife, but in cities they have even more benefits, from cooling their surroundings, absorbing polluting particles and preventing flooding, to reducing crime and road rage (yes, really!). The more trees we plant, the more comfortable and healthy our cities will be to live in, now and in the future.

According to the United Nations, more than 50 per cent of people live in cities now, with nearly 70 per cent of the world's human population expected to live in cities by 2050. Urban areas are warmer than rural areas because there are more hard, dark surfaces to absorb heat from the sun – every pavement, road and wall acts as a storage heater. What's more, the structure of some cities – particularly those with narrow streets and tall buildings – prevents heat from being released, as there's little opportunity for natural wind flow. Human activity in cities also contributes to urban heating, with motorised vehicles, buildings and (ironically) air-conditioning units all creating "waste heat".

This absorption of heat contributes to what's known as the "Heat Island Effect", with some cities already dramatically warmer than their rural counterparts. Warmer cities might not seem so bad now, but a 2019 study predicts a 2°C (4°F) global rise by 2050 will see city temperatures rise exponentially higher. In the hottest months, these temperature increases will not only affect people's ability to work, but will dramatically affect their ability to live well, with those with asthma and heart issues most at risk.

Cooling effects

Trees, and plants generally, are cooler than pavements and walls. If you've ever walked into a woodland on a hot summer's day you will have felt the immediate relief of the sudden drop in temperature as you entered a world that instantly refreshed you.

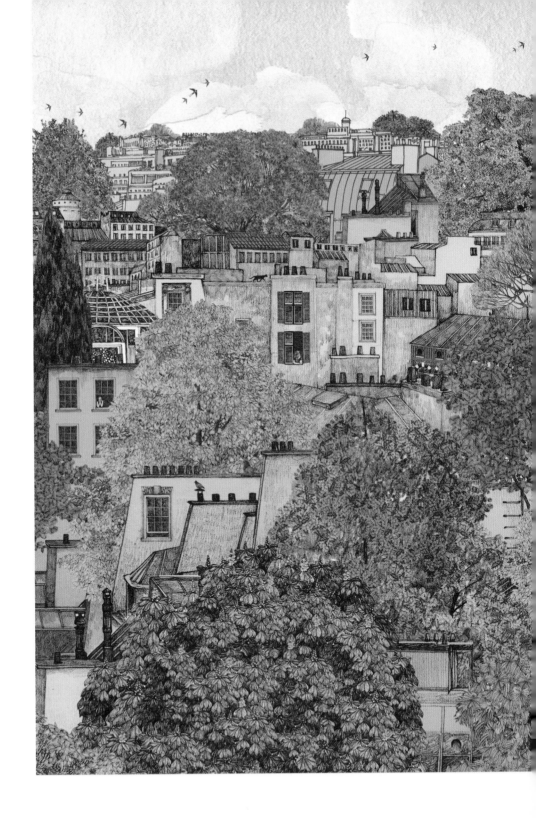

Growing more trees and plants will help reduce urban heating, as each tree creates shade and prevents sunlight from hitting hard surfaces. Tree roots will also absorb water and so reduce the risk of flooding, while the leaves will absorb pollution particles and help clean the air. The shade cast by tree canopies provides a break from the heat, while leaves, bark, branches, flowers and berries provide food and homes for wildlife.

We should all, therefore, be planting trees in every available park, tree pit (a hole made for a street tree) and bit of waste ground across our cities, now. We should also be planting ivy and other climbers up walls of buildings, adding green roofs and balcony gardens wherever we can. Remember that, as well as deflecting heat, every single leaf absorbs carbon dioxide, every root holds onto water.

Planting street trees

As lovely as street trees are, the sad truth is that planting them can be complicated and expensive. Street trees usually need to be planted with root barrier systems to prevent their roots disrupting cables and pipes beneath pavements, which provide electricity, Wi-Fi and water to businesses and homes. They need to have grates fitted to stop the roots becoming compacted by city footfall, or creating trip hazards on the pavement surface. They need to be planted on wide pavements to ensure full access for those in wheelchairs. Ideally, and sadly, they should not be fruiting (female) trees, as fruit creates a mess, as well as a potential slip hazard, when it falls to the ground. Male trees produce valuable pollen for the pollinators that are around, but the pollen may cause issues for people with hayfever.

What's more, street trees need regular watering to keep them alive (at least in their first couple of years), and pruning to make sure they don't encroach on the road, or drop branches. In autumn they need their leaves collecting and disposing of.

Do trees like being street trees? Do they enjoy having their roots restricted and not connected to other trees, their canopies pruned into regimented shapes, their pollen floating around the city with few female flowers to fertilise? I think, on balance, the answer has to be: no. We know trees are communal species. We know they do best when growing together in groups, that they connect to each other and

UNDERSTANDING TREES

share information and even keep each other alive through the power of their connected root systems, aided by fungi (see p.22). Some studies have also shown that street trees absorb less carbon dioxide than those growing in more natural environments.

I like street trees: they make me happy and I love a tree-lined street. But, given the huge cost of planting and maintaining them, plus the fact that it's perhaps not the best option for the trees themselves, I think we should look for other ways to "reforest" our cities.

Alternatives to street trees

We could start with planting small copses in parks, where there are fewer, if any, cables and pipes to be mindful of, and unrestricted ground where tree roots can connect as they would in the wild. We should look at areas of waste ground and see if groups of trees can be planted there, with small urban forests popping up across our cities.

Existing street trees should be looked after and tree-lined streets celebrated. Empty tree pits, where a street tree once grew, should be replanted, as there will already be no cables or pipes to be mindful of. Perhaps city planners and road builders can look at ways we can bring trees to our streets without growing them in such stressful conditions. Instead of tree-lined streets, we can have tree-rich corners, with small groups of trees on areas of bare ground. Perhaps we can find spaces for urban hedges and climbers where trees won't grow. We can also, of course, plant trees in urban gardens. There's absolutely nothing stopping us from doing that.

We should be planting trees in every available park, tree pit and bit of waste urban ground, now.

PLANT ONE TREE

A tree is a remarkable thing. From root to branch, through the seasonal cycles of blossom and fruit, to the glorious displays of deciduous autumn colour, a single tree can transform a garden and captivate us year after year. Find out how these amazing lifecycle stages can be put to use in your garden, and make your tree an intrinsic part of it.

Parts of a tree

So far, I've talked about the big picture: the evolution of trees, their community, their role in rewilding and in our cities. But what, exactly, is a tree? Botanically speaking, it's a woody plant that lives for many years, characterised by its tall (usually single) trunk, bark and branches. Each tree has evolved independently to compete for sunlight, so it can photosynthesise (make its own food, using sunlight).

Superficially, trees are made of the roots, trunk and crown – which includes stems, twigs and leaves.

Roots

The roots absorb water and nutrients from the soil, store nutrients and anchor the tree into the earth. Tree roots are typically shallow. They're mostly found in the top 60cm (2ft) of the soil and rarely penetrate deeper than about 2m (6½ft). However, some trees have a taproot (a long, single root that penetrates into the soil) to reach deep for extra sources of water and nutrients.

Tree roots usually spread around two to three times the radius of the tree's canopy. As the tree grows, any taproot recedes in size while the lateral (side) roots thicken and become woody, eventually protruding from the soil. Many trees depend on a symbiotic relationship between their roots and mycorrhizal fungi (see p.22), which aids the absorption of water and nutrients.

Trunk

The trunk comprises several parts, some of which transport food and nutrients. At the centre is the heartwood, which is the core of the tree and its strongest part. While it is not technically living, the core will retain its strength as long as the outer layers of the trunk are intact.

Around the heartwood is the sapwood, which contains vascular xylem tissues that transport watery fluid (known as sap, and containing minerals and other nutrients) from the tree's roots to the branches and leaves. As the tree matures, the older

Parts of a tree

sapwood becomes heartwood. On the outside of the trunk is the woody bark, which protects the inner parts. Only the inner layers of bark are alive, with new bark produced by a vascular system of cells known as the cambium.

The inner bark layer is called the phloem, and, when young, contains vascular tissues that transport food (glucose) in sap from the leaves to the branches, fruit, trunk and roots of the tree. As the phloem matures, it turns to cork, giving way to newer material to carry nutrients around the tree.

Crown

The crown of the tree is made up of its branches and leaves. The leaves produce glucose (sugar), via the process of photosynthesis. This involves using energy from the sun, which is absorbed using chlorophyll in each leaf cell; chlorophyll also gives the leaf its green colour. The sun's energy is used to split water molecules into their hydrogen and oxygen atoms. The hydrogen is then combined with carbon dioxide to create glucose, which is transported to provide nutrients for other areas of the tree. The oxygen is released back into the atmosphere.

How trees grow

Trees absorb water through their roots and make food in their leaves. They grow by producing new cells, but only in certain parts of the tree, called meristems (unlike animals, where cell production can occur in most parts of the body).

Trees have meristems on their branch tips, root tips, leaf and flower buds, and in the vascular cambium, which produces new phloem and xylem cells each year, particularly in regions with pronounced seasons. This causes the trunk, branches and roots to increase in diameter seasonally (which is how you can "age" a tree from its "growth rings"). So trees grow outwards and upwards, but only from their tips and outer edges. Most tree growth occurs in the warmth and light of spring and summer, but growth may also be halted during periods of drought or extreme heat.

How deciduous trees survive

In autumn, deciduous trees shed their delicate leaves (see p.42) and enter into a period of dormancy. In dormancy, immature leaves (and sometimes flowers) are held in a protective bud until temperatures increase and they can continue growing without risk of frost damage. Late frosts can affect spring blossom, however, particularly on early-flowering fruit trees.

How evergreen trees keep their leaves

Evergreen trees have evolved to produce glossy or needle-like leaves, which are much more resilient to winter temperatures than the soft leaves of deciduous trees. Evergreens continue to photosynthesise during winter but at a much slower rate.

What's more, some evergreens produce a sort of "antifreeze" to help the tree through winter. When water freezes it expands and takes up more space, so it can burst the cells of fragile leaves. The evergreens' "antifreeze" comprises a series of hormones and proteins, which keep cell walls intact.

Shrubs

You may see a tree described as a shrub or small tree, which means that it can be grown as either. Hawthorn and elder fall into this category. Generally speaking, shrubs are multi-stemmed, woody plants with a rounded shape, whereas trees are taller and have a single stem. However the definitions aren't that simple, as you can have multi-stemmed trees, such as magnolias, and small trees that can also be grown as shrubs, or as hedging plants, such as hawthorn and elder.

How you grow or prune the plant can determine whether it develops into a tree or shrub. In my garden I grow a standard hawthorn tree, but I also have a hawthorn that I'm growing as a hedging plant and another that I'm growing as a shrub.

Trees grow outwards and upwards, but only from their tips and outer edges.

Your tree through the year

Thinking about how your tree will look from spring to winter may help you decide which to choose. In addition to size and shape and how it fits into your garden and among other plants (see pp.154–55), think about how it will look in different seasons. It's worth considering not only flowers and fruits, but also bark in autumn and winter, and spring catkins and autumn leaf colour.

Deciduous trees are bare in winter, may be smothered in blossom in spring and fruit in summer, and their leaves may turn shades of red, yellow, orange and even purple before falling in autumn. Evergreen trees retain their leaves, so are less varied through the year, but they may bear flowers and fruits over the seasons.

Spring
Spring comes with rising temperatures and sap, as trees (and the rest of the garden) burst into growth. Leaves unfurl and flowers open, offering potentially dazzling displays of blossom and/or new leaves, which can be a different colour to mature leaves. Many trees are renowned for their spring blossom (see pp.38–39) – fruit trees such as apple, pear and cherry are particularly beautiful, with some having ornamental varieties with even greater amounts of blossom. As well as these fruiting trees, others that boast incredible spring flowers include blackthorn, hawthorn, juneberry and elderflower. Willows are also worth a mention, as some varieties (such as the Kilmarnock willow) bear spectacular spring catkins which are loved by bees.

Summer
Trees are full of leaf in summer, and some have immature fruits developing. As with winter, summer is normally not a season of spectacular displays, although it's important to take time to appreciate the tree in all its leafy glory, and to get outside to listen to the rustle of those wonderful leaves before they fall. It's also vital to

consider the tree as a backdrop to other plants. A solid green can be the perfect foil for other colours, so you might plant a flowering shrub, such as weigela, in front of it. Some trees, such as crape myrtle and varieties of dogwood, flower in summer, so if you're after a dazzling summer display there is some choice available.

Autumn

A time of glorious leaf colour, autumn is when deciduous trees start to enter dormancy (see pp.42–43). Fruiting trees are at their fruitiest in autumn, too, and some species, such as crab apples, boast autumn leaf colour and fruits at the same time. For the best trees for autumn colour look no further than Japanese maples, stag's horn sumach, beech, sweet gum, Chinese tupelo and maidenhair tree (see also pp.124–35).

Winter

In winter, deciduous trees have bare stems, with small leaf and/or flower buds ready to burst into growth in spring. While the skeletal frame of a deciduous tree in winter is a thing of beauty in its own right, in a small space you might consider one with striking bark, such as Tibetan cherry, paperbark maple and Himalayan birch. These can form the perfect winter focal point if grown in a prominent position in the garden.

In a small space you may also plump for an evergreen tree. Evergreen trees largely look the same throughout the year, but some will retain fruit or berries during the winter, adding to their appeal (and their wildlife value). The strawberry tree is a particular highlight, bearing flowers and fruit in winter, while retaining its glossy evergreen leaves.

The skeletal frame of a deciduous tree in winter is a thing of beauty.

Spring blossom

One of the most fantastic displays the natural world has to offer is spring blossom. After months of winter, along comes spring with its masses of blousy pink and white flowers. Stand beneath a fruit tree in full blossom and you will hear nothing but the buzz of bees as they zoom from one pollen-loaded flower to another. Spring blossom is life-giving, life-affirming stuff.

While lots of trees flower in spring, "blossom" typically refers to the flowers of trees in the Rosaceae family, which includes apples, cherries, peaches and pears.

Celebrating blossom

Cherry blossom is particularly celebrated – it's the national flower of Japan and thousands of people gather together each spring for *hanami*, or to "view the cherry trees". There are hundreds of varieties of ornamental and fruiting cherries. Most ornamentals are cultivars of the Japanese cherry *Prunus cerasus* (or "sakura"). While beautiful, many have double flowers, meaning bees and other pollinators have difficulty accessing the pollen and nectar.

Although cherry blossom is undoubtedly lovely, it's apple blossom that I love the most. In a good year, apple and crab apple trees are so covered in blossom you can barely see the stems. Most varieties have pink buds that open to pink-blushed white flowers. From a distance they look like fluffy cumulus clouds, and close up they roar with the buzz of hundreds of queen bumblebees. To plant a blossom tree in your garden is to plant a firm seasonal marker. You'll spend winter looking for signs of bud burst, and spring marvelling at its flowers.

Despite not officially being blossom trees, other flowering trees are not to be sniffed at. The juneberry bears beautiful spring flowers, as does the eastern redbud. Magnolias are also renowned for their variety of gorgeous spring flowers. Just don't call them blossom!

Spring blossom

Fruit, nuts, seeds and berries

Adding colour, interest and wildlife value, fruit, nuts, seeds and berries enhance a tree's garden appeal. While many gardeners plump for a fruiting or berrying tree, don't underestimate the beauty of a seeding tree like birch or alder. I love to watch blue tits hanging upside down to eat from my silver birch tree – the seeds might not be that colourful, but the birds are!

Trees, like all plants, reproduce by fertilisation, a process that enables them to produce seed for the next generation. Fertilisation occurs after pollination, when male pollen comes into contact with female ovaries. Tree flowers are pollinated by insects or wind – fertilised flowers develop into fruit, which takes several forms, including berries, nuts and cones.

Insect pollination

Many trees, such as apples, cherries and hawthorn, produce sweet, sugary nectar to attract pollinating insects. Pollinators have different mouthparts. The proboscis (tongue) length varies between bees, butterflies and moths, while flies have a different type of proboscis altogether. Flowers of all kinds have evolved various shapes to accommodate different mouths. Insect-pollinated trees can have male and female flowers on the same tree or on separate trees. Some flowers contain male and female parts within the same bloom; these are known as hermaphrodites. This doesn't always mean they are self-fertile, however. You may be familiar with the need for a "pollination partner" for apple trees (see p.151). This is because, despite having hermaphrodite flowers, many apple trees still need to be cross-pollinated with another tree.

When insects visit flowers, they either collect pollen intentionally, or it "accidentally" attaches to their body as they are feeding on nectar. The more flowers they visit, the more pollen is transferred on and off their bodies. Some bees are particularly good at pollination: honeybees and bumblebees comb pollen off their bodies into neat "baskets" on their hind legs, but others carry pollen in a rough "brush" on their abdomen. This increases the chance of pollen falling from their body as they visit new flowers, resulting in fertilisation.

Wind pollination

Some trees, including oaks, release pollen into the air in the hope that wind will carry it to the ovaries. Conifers are also wind-pollinated, but they bear male and female cones instead of flowers.

How fruits, nuts, seeds and berries form

After fertilisation, the female flower parts develop into a fruit containing seeds. The fruit can be fleshy, like a berry, apple or cherry, or papery and winged like a samara (on sycamores, birches and elms). As trees can't move, they have evolved ways for their seeds to travel to a variety of places. Fruits and berries can be eaten by a mammal or bird, and the seed dispersed to grow elsewhere – potentially miles from the original tree. Samaras can be lifted and carried on the wind. Some fruits, such as coconuts, float on water and can start a new generation on a different land mass.

Many "nuts", including almonds and walnuts, are actually fruits known as drupes – the part we eat is the seed, which is within a fleshy layer. True nuts, such as hazelnuts, acorns and chestnuts, are botanically described as dry, single-seeded fruits. They are formed when the ovary wall of a fertilised flower hardens into a tough shell. The same fertilisation process results in so many different outcomes. Isn't nature amazing?

Flowers have evolved various shapes to accommodate different mouths of pollinators.

Autumn leaf colour

Planting a tree for autumn colour is planting light in darkness. Just as the flowers fade and the garden starts to recede, along comes the tree with a whole new colour palette. I love my silver birch most in autumn, when its heart-shaped leaves turn a glorious buttery yellow. It's the first thing I see when I look out of the window, and when the sun catches its leaves my heart melts a little.

Besides the silver birch, my hawthorn and rowan provide colour with fat, red berries, and the hawthorn sometimes displays red leaves, too. But many deciduous trees look good in autumn, with oranges, reds and yellows dominating as a final flourish before winter sets in.

The orange and yellow pigments in leaves are actually present all year round, but we can't see them because they're hidden by the dominant green pigment, chlorophyll, which is needed for photosynthesis to make glucose (food for the tree). Some leaves also contain red-pink pigments (anthocyanins), which are equally hidden by the chlorophyll.

Towards the end of summer, the tree stops producing chlorophyll, and no longer relies on photosynthesis as a source of energy, using stored glucose instead. As the leaves die back, the green pigments break down first to reveal the other hidden pigments. The intensity and stability of the red-pink pigments differ according to how much glucose a tree has stored, soil acidity, temperature and other factors. This means that autumn colour can vary widely from year to year.

At this point the leaves are no longer working to produce food for the tree. The vessels that connect the leaf to the tree are closed off and a layer of cells between the leaf stalk and the twig holding it, known as the abscission layer, increases in size. This process severs the leaf from its twig without leaving a wound. The tree enters dormancy, saving its energy over winter for the its next big moment: spring.

The tree's role in your garden

The tree in your garden will have three key roles: one for you and those who live with you, including your neighbours; one for the other trees, plants and fungi growing around it; and one for the wildlife – from the tiniest insects such as aphids and leafminers, to the birds that land in its branches and the small mammals that rest in its holes and hibernate beneath its fallen leaves.

People root themselves to their garden tree. They mark the seasons by its different looks: spring by masses of blossom, autumn by leaf colour and/or fruit, winter by a skeleton frame or vivid bark or (if it's evergreen) glossy leaves and berries.

The tree and you
Noticing changes in a tree over the seasons is mindful. This mindfulness helps distract us from other things that may be dragging us down, and helps improve our mental health. Watching each season unfold reminds us that the world is still turning, that these ancient natural processes, of bud burst and flowering and fruiting and leaf fall, are still intact.

You might sit beneath your tree and listen to its leaves rustling or its sap rising. You might watch birds perch on its branches or squirrels scamper up and down its trunk. When its leaves fall in autumn you might spot blackbirds turning them over in search of grubs. You might stand, transfixed, as a robin stuffs berries into its mouth.

Planting a tree is the ultimate in self care because, from the moment you plant it, you will never stop being in love with its processes, its stature, its function in the garden. To plant a tree is to invest in the future, yes, but to plant a tree is also to invest in yourself. Because trees are inherently good for you.

And it's not just you who will benefit from it – your neighbours, too, some of whom you will never have met, may love your tree. They too will track its seasons, its autumn colour and spring blossom. They too will enjoy the birds your tree brings, for they won't land in your garden alone, but in other gardens, too. Don't forget that, in planting your tree you're providing a service for your community (see pp.50–51) – just as people will stop to admire a pretty front garden, so they will enjoy a tree, even from a couple of streets away.

More practically, your tree will provide shade from the hottest sun, add height and structure to your garden, and create a focal point. You might plant it in front of an unsightly building you want to hide, or in a position that blocks your view of a neighbour's window, giving you more privacy. More practical still, it will hold water in the earth with its roots, doing its small part to avert flooding. If you plant your tree in an urban area it will contribute to the cooling of city temperatures (see pp.26–28). The leaves of your tree will also buffer wind and absorb polluting particles, something we will benefit from now, and in years to come.

The tree and your garden

Trees connect with other trees, shrubs and plants via their root systems and the fungal threads (hyphae) that grow around them (see p.22). Trees do better when planted in small groups as they feed and communicate with each other via their root systems, aided by fungi. If you do have room to plant more than one tree then please do. If not, perhaps your neighbour has a tree, which yours can connect with?

The tree and wildlife

The best trees for wildlife provide a range of different food types and habitats for a wide variety of species, including insects and their larvae, and birds.

Native trees tend to be better for wildlife than non-natives (see pp.20–21). Moths and other flying insects can lay eggs on the leaves, and birds will take the resulting larvae and feed them to their chicks in the nest. As your tree grows it might develop fissures in its bark, which can shelter hibernating insects. As it ages, holes will appear in the trunk, which will provide nesting sites for birds and small mammals. Gaps between the roots might fill with water and provide the perfect habitat for hoverflies to lay their eggs, while a dry hole might be large enough for a hedgehog. A tree is an ecosystem in its own right, a city that hundreds of species might call home.

Finding the right spot

Before you reach for the spade to plant your tree, you'll need to think about the impact it will have on you and your neighbours. Pay attention to where the light falls in the garden, how much shade will be cast in yours and your neighbours' spaces. Don't just think about the tree – and the garden – now, but also how they will change over the next 20 years or more.

It's a sad fact that trees and hedges are a frequent cause of neighbourly disputes. Common complaints arise from hedges and trees growing too tall and casting too much shade, while those that drop a lot of leaves or seeds can be problematic, too. The last thing you want is to fall out with your neighbours, so plan carefully. It may be worth chatting with them beforehand: they might offer some advice, or even be inspired to plant a tree of their own!

Think about shade
Depending on where the sun hits your garden, planting your tree on one side or end of the space means it could cast less shade on neighbouring plots. If you think shade is likely to be an issue, avoid trees with large, dense canopies (such as evergreens). Trees with an airy canopy, such as silver birch and some types of palm, cast only dappled shade rather than deep shade, so can be a happy compromise in a built-up area.

It's also worth thinking about how much shade is already cast in your garden. Most trees eventually grow to a height where their leaves can access the sun (it's how they evolved to be trees in the first place), so planting a tree on the north-facing side of your garden won't be a problem in the long term – if a fence casts shade, your tree will easily grow beyond it. However, buildings and other trees cast shade that could block much-needed light from your tree. Some trees are more tolerant of shade than others – typically flowering and fruiting trees need a lot of sun to help ripen their fruits, but foliage trees can cope with less light. Bear in mind, however, that the best autumn colours result from trees that have had a lot of summer sun (see p.42).

Planting near buildings

Trees near buildings don't usually cause damage, but some can. Tree roots can affect drains and paving, or in rare cases cause subsidence, while branches can affect roofs and guttering. Subsidence is more likely with houses built before the 1950s, as they have shallower foundations than those built today. This is most likely if you have clay soil, which can shrink in prolonged periods of drought. Older houses also have older drainage systems, making it more likely that tree roots can enter and block them.

In the UK, there are no rules on the distance a tree should be planted from a house. How far you plant your tree from your house should depend on how old the house is, and the type of tree you choose. A fruit tree grafted onto a dwarfing rootstock will not have the root run of a mighty oak, and will never grow as tall as your roof and guttering. But large deciduous trees, particularly those with suckering roots, such as elm, should be avoided.

As a general rule, trees extend their roots out to the equivalent distance of between half and the whole tree's height. More drought-tolerant trees have less reliance on water and so have smaller root systems. Look at the eventual height of your tree, its drought tolerance, your soil type and the age of your house, and do what's best for you. I planted my trees 12m (40ft) from my Victorian house, but the rowan is only 5m (16ft) from my neighbours' new-build. Its canopy could grow to up to 8m (26ft) after 50 years (4m/13ft on either side of the trunk), and some branches may need to be pruned annually to protect guttering. On my loamy soil the roots won't be an issue.

Integrating the tree into your garden

It's also important to consider how your tree will affect the look of your garden. Over time, it will become a huge presence, adding height and structure, becoming a focal point that will draw your eye across the garden. Use this to your advantage – create an attractive border around the tree (see pp.154–55), adding shrubs and herbaceous plants that will not only look good, but will grow in harmony with your tree as well as providing additional habitats for birds, bees and other wildlife.

Choose a tree that fits the scale of your garden: a full-sized tree isn't always the best option. The space may be too small or shady, or your neighbours may have already shown concern at the potential shade cast on their garden. Luckily there are some alternatives to consider.

Hedging

A hedge is a wonderful thing, made simply by planting trees very close together (at 30cm/12in intervals) and cutting them back every one to two years. In small spaces, you can maintain a height of just a metre (3ft), and plant in single rows so the hedge doesn't grow too wide. Or, if you have more room, plant in double rows for a thicker hedge, and let it grow to a height of 2m (6½ft) or more.

Hedges are great for small urban spaces, not only because they can be trimmed to size, but because they can absorb more polluting particles than trees as they grow closer to the ground (the perfect height to absorb particles from cars). They still absorb carbon dioxide and drink water, and they have wildlife value, too. Hedges provide a natural boundary to gardens and enable wildlife to travel more easily between them, while also offering shelter for anything from nesting birds to hibernating hedgehogs. What's more, hedges filter the wind, helping to slow it down. Such a wind break can be a godsend in exposed gardens, and could provide a great solution to windier conditions caused by climate change.

Some trees lend themselves better to hedging than others – evergreen trees such as yew make particularly dense hedges, while regular trimming keeps beech trees in their juvenile state, so their autumn leaves remain on throughout winter, to beautiful effect. A mixed native hedge of hawthorn, hazel, blackthorn and field rose makes a wonderful wildlife habitat, providing food and homes for a huge range of species.

Espalier and fan-trained trees

Fan-trained and espalier trees are usually fruit trees grown against a wall or fence, trained as either a fan shape or as a series of "tiers" known as an espalier. They are a fantastic way to grow fruit in a small space, and they are gloriously ornamental. You can even grow fan- and espalier-trained trees on wires between posts. I have such an "espalier boundary" between mine and my neighbours' allotment plots. Between us, we have two apple and three pear trees, and we share the fruit each year.

Apples and pears can be trained in a number of ways, including as fans and espaliers. Cherries, peaches, plums and apricots are fan-trained only (see p.151). All are sold either as whips (young trees) that you train yourself or as pre-trained trees you can plant and then prune annually. They're all easy to grow and produce a surprising amount of fruit.

Growing trees in pots

If you have a really small space, live in rented accommodation or have very poor soil, you could grow a tree in a pot. Only very small trees are suitable, but some have been developed for this purpose. Apples grown on dwarfing rootstocks do well in pots, while slow-growing Japanese maples and flowering dogwoods make fantastic ornamental choices. For a formal, evergreen display choose olive, yew or bay, or for a sunny, sheltered site you might go for a lemon or fig. A tree's root run in a pot will never match that of free ground, so you will need to water and feed it regularly to ensure it grows well. Mulching or replacing the top few centimetres of soil annually will keep soil fresh.

Climbers

In even smaller spaces, if you can't fit in another tree, and hedges aren't an option, look to climbers. Most are easy to grow and can be as tall and dense as trees and hedges. Ivy has incredible value, absorbing pollutants and providing homes for wildlife. Honeysuckle and clematis, climbing and rambling roses, and jasmine are other possibilities.

A mixed native hedge of hawthorn, hazel, blackthorn and field rose makes a wonderful wildlife habitat.

The tree in the community

According to the Office for National Statistics (ONS), one in eight homes has no garden. So, if you don't have a garden, how do you plant a tree? In your community, of course! You can join a community group, set one up, or get involved in planting trees in a local park or green space.

There are thousands of community groups across the country. Some use pockets of land for communal gardens and nature reserves, while others help maintain parks. I've seen allotments on old railway tracks, "secret gardens" in church grounds, and planting groups on corners of pavement. Even planters on your high street can be used to green your area.

Joining a community group

If you want to get involved with your community, find out what groups already exist. Look for "Friends of" groups, covering all sorts from parks to nature reserves, small community gardens, allotments and squares. Check your local area's Facebook page, ask the council, or visit your park or green space to see if there are posters advertising such a group. You can set up your own with advice from your council or another group.

Planting in a communal space

There are other options apart from a group. Contact your council's arboreal (tree) team. You may be able to "donate" a tree to a local park, which the arboreal team plants and maintains for a fee. Planting in green spaces such as parks and community gardens is much easier and cheaper than street trees (see pp.28–29), but consult your council first. They will let you know if there are cables underground or access is needed, and they'll also need to know as it's likely that they will maintain them. Never plant trees without permission – you could be creating a headache for someone later down the line.

TREE PROFILES

If you plant only one tree, make sure it's the right one for you and your garden. Discover fifty garden trees, with options for spring blossom and other flowers, berries, fruits and seeds, plus evergreens and palms. You'll also find ideas for large and small outdoor spaces, along with tips for helping wildlife and growing trees in a changing climate.

SMALL
TREES

For those of us with smaller gardens and outdoor spaces, as well as urban gardens where plot size, shade and neighbours are considerations, small trees are an obvious choice. Many can be grown in containers on patios, roof gardens and balconies. Small trees come in a variety of shapes and sizes and can be evergreen or deciduous, flowering and/or fruiting, good for wildlife and highly ornamental. While a few trees in this selection can grow as tall as 12m (39ft) tall (most are much smaller), they are slow-growing and may take many years to reach this size. You'll find small trees in other categories, too, such as Fruit trees (see pp.64–77) and Trees for autumn colour (see pp.124–35).

Leaf

Twig

Berries

SNOWY MESPILUS

Amelanchier lamarckii

An attractively shaped, often multi-stemmed, tree, snowy mespilus has coppery pink young leaves bursting just as masses of snow-white, star-shaped flowers appear in spring.

Snowy mespilus works well as a feature in a lawn or as part of a mixed ornamental border or hedge. The leaves mature to a yellow-green before turning vivid shades of red in autumn. The red-purple berries are used to decorate desserts such as muffins, pies and cheesecakes in North America. They are also popular with garden birds.

There are several hybrid cultivars of snowy mespilus, including *Amelanchier × grandiflora* 'Ballerina', which has a more upright habit than *A. lamarckii*, and *A. × grandiflora* 'Robin Hill', which has beautiful pink flowers.

ID NOTES

Leaves Oblong, papery, tinted bronze in spring; red in autumn

Twigs Reddish, with occasional grey mottling

Flowers Star-shaped, white

Fruit Dark red-purple edible berries

Bark Smooth and grey with faint lines and grey spots developing with age

CARE NOTES

Grow in full sun for the best flowering, fruiting and autumn colour. If growing as a hedge, plant 2m (6½ft) apart. Snowy mespilus doesn't need regular pruning but it pays to remove dead or crossing stems after flowering. Mulch in autumn with home-made compost or well-rotted manure.

Height/spread 12x8m (39x26ft) after 20 years

Life expectancy 40 years

Soil type Clay, loam, sand; acid or neutral; moist but well-drained

Native to North America

Hardiness H7

ID NOTES

Leaves Up to 6cm (2½in) long, glossy and oval with rounded teeth; in autumn usually yellow but sometimes red, orange and purple

Twigs Greyish, developing cracks with age, bearing pointed leaf buds with fine, downy hairs on short stalks; twigs may sometimes develop spines in exposed areas

Flowers Five petals and may be white, pink or red

Fruit/seed Small, apple-like fruits, usually red or yellow

Bark Grey-brown, flecked

Leaf

Twig

Flower

Fruit

Malus sylvestris

CRAB APPLE

Malus **spp.**

Perfect for small gardens, crab apples are compact and look good almost all year. In spring, they bear masses of blossom, which develops into colourful autumn fruits that last well into winter. Some species have dramatic autumn foliage, too. Crab apples are excellent for wildlife, with flowers and fruit used by a variety of species. They're also handy for gardeners – they're often grown as a "pollination partner" (see p.151) for edible apples to help them produce more fruit.

Most crab apples can be grown as a large shrub or small tree, with some species bearing double flowers or unusual leaf colouring. They really are gorgeous trees.

Crab apple blossom is invaluable to pollinators – particularly bees – and the fruit of many varieties is used to make crab apple jelly. Any fruit left on the tree provides food for birds and small mammals in winter. Crab apples can also host mistletoe, a semi-parasitic plant that grows in the bark of some species. In the British Isles there is one native crab apple, *Malus sylvestris*, which is usually grown as a tree but is also used in hedging. There are around 40 other crab apple species native to Europe, Asia and North America, including *M. sargentii* and *M. floribunda*, which are both multi-stemmed. Most trees available to buy are derived from one or more of these species.

CARE NOTES

Only light pruning is usually necessary for trees, with the removal of dead and crossing stems a priority (see p.159). Some species benefit from the lowest stems being removed to "lift" the canopy. Crab apples are susceptible to a number of pests and diseases including apple scab, fireblight, codling moth and cedar-apple rust. Usually the tree can live quite happily while affected, and there's no need to take any action. Pests such as aphids are part of the natural ecosystem and will be eaten by predators such as birds and wasps.

Height/spread 5x4m (16x13ft) after 20 years

Life expectancy 70 years

Soil type Clay, loam, sand; acid, alkaline or neutral; moist but well-drained

Native to Europe, North America, Asia

Hardiness H6

BRONZE LOQUAT

Eriobotrya deflexa

Highly ornamental if you're after a tropical look, bronze loquat has evergreen growth that gives it year-round appeal in small spaces.

It has a neat, compact habit, making it ideal for growing in pots, or training as a standard or even as an espalier tree (see p.151). Its dense canopy means it can also make a good screen. The leathery leaves can grow to 30cm (12in), and have almost white undersides. As well as having striking leaves, bronze loquat produces small flowers and may bear medlar-like fruit. In Britain, the summers aren't warm enough for the fruit to ripen enough to be edible, unless it is unusually hot. However, with climate change, growing your own loquat fruit could be on the cards in future.

Leaf

Flower

Fruit

Height/spread 8x8m (26x26ft) after 20 years

Life expectancy 30–50 years

Soil type Chalk, clay, loam, sand; acid, alkaline or neutral; moist but well-drained

Native to China and Japan

Hardiness H4

ID NOTES

Leaves Evergreen glossy, oblong and green, up to 20cm (8in) long; felted undersides

Twigs Green and thick

Flowers Small and pink-white, borne in panicles with a hawthorn-like scent

Fruit/seed Fuzzy, edible fruit like a cross between apples and apricots, with a sharp taste

Bark Thin and easily damaged

CARE NOTES

Hardy to -10°C (14°F), bronze loquat may suffer damage in winter. Have some horticultural fleece handy to protect the leaves if temperatures dip below -10°C (14°F), or, if growing in a pot, move indoors until temperatures increase again.

SOFT TREE FERN

Dicksonia antarctica

Tree ferns are not strictly trees, but with their trunk-like stems and crown of fronds, they look like them, and play the same role in the garden.

A tree fern's "trunk" is actually its root system, and is covered in masses of aerial roots, which take much of the tree's water and nutrients from the humid atmosphere. This means, in dry conditions, you may have to water the trunk to keep it moist.

Tree ferns are extremely slow growing – 2.5cm (1in) per year – so buy as mature a specimen as you can afford. They work well in urban spaces, including courtyards, and as part of a woodland planting scheme (with an exotic twist!). Despite being native to Tasmania, which rarely has temperatures below freezing, tree ferns are hardy to -9°C (16°F) for short periods, although they will lose their leaves, and it's important to ensure the trunk doesn't freeze. For the best chance of survival, grow them in a humid, shady spot.

ID NOTES

Leaves Fern-like fronds

Fruit/seed Doesn't produce seeds, but has tiny spores on the undersides of the fronds

Bark Matted, fibrous network of roots

CARE NOTES

In winter, protect the trunk and growing point at the top by wrapping them in the old fronds, along with some straw and horticultural fleece. This will stop the tree's root system from freezing or drying out, and should ensure new fronds sprout from the top of the tree in spring.

Height/spread 2.5x2m (8x6½ft) after 20–50 years

Life expectancy 500 years

Soil type Clay, loam; neutral or acid; boggy, moist

Native to Tasmania

Hardiness H3

Trunk

Frond

OLIVE

Olea europaea

One of the oldest known cultivated trees, the olive was traditionally grown for its fruit as well as being a symbol of happiness and peace. The average lifespan of olive trees is 300–600 years, with the oldest recorded at 2,000 years old. Olives make popular evergreen garden trees in southern regions of Britain, bearing silvery grey, oval leaves, inconspicuous white flowers and, occasionally, edible olives.

Olives are highly ornamental and easy to grow. They do best – and are more likely to produce fruit – in sun, and they tolerate poor soils. Slow growing, they do well in pots. You can train an olive as a standard – with a long single stem; a pair of standards looks good on either side of a doorway. In colder areas they may need winter protection.

Olives are wind pollinated. If you're lucky, your olive tree may start producing fruit after three to five years. You can harvest the olives when they're green but it's best if you can wait until they're black and starting to fall from the branches.

Freshly harvested olives are bitter to taste. To make them palatable, simply soak the olives in water for ten days, changing the water every day. Store them in jars of brine (salted water) for about four weeks before eating.

CARE NOTES

Very little pruning is needed. However, in late spring or early summer, remove dead, diseased or dying branches (see pp.158–59). For standard trees, treat your olive as any other fruit tree, thinning out branches to create an open, bowl-shaped centre, where light and air can reach developing fruit. Avoid pruning too hard as this will result in non-fruiting "water shoots", which are weaker and more susceptible to disease than regular branches.

For winter protection of olives in pots, if needed, you can buy a fleece jacket that you pop over the crown of the tree like a bag, then tighten around the stem with a drawstring.

Height/spread 8 x 3m (26x10ft) after 20 years

Life expectancy 300 years

Soil type Clay, loam, sand; acid, alkaline or neutral; moist but well-drained

Native to Europe

Hardiness H4

TREE PROFILES

ID NOTES

Leaves Leathery, silvery grey-green, oval and narrow, up to 7.5cm (3in) long

Twigs Smooth and grey

Flowers Tiny and white, borne in racemes up to 5cm (2in) long

Fruit Green drupes (olives), ripening to black, with a central stone

Bark Smooth and grey when young, ageing to rugged and gnarled

Fruit

Bark

Flower

ID NOTES

Leaves Oval and glossy, up to 12cm (5in) long; yellow, red and purple in autumn

Twigs Light brown and slightly fuzzy

Flowers Red, borne in tight clusters on bare stems

Fruit Woody seed capsules contain a single, shiny brown seed, and split open when ripe

Bark Smooth, maturing to flaking in grey, cream and orange

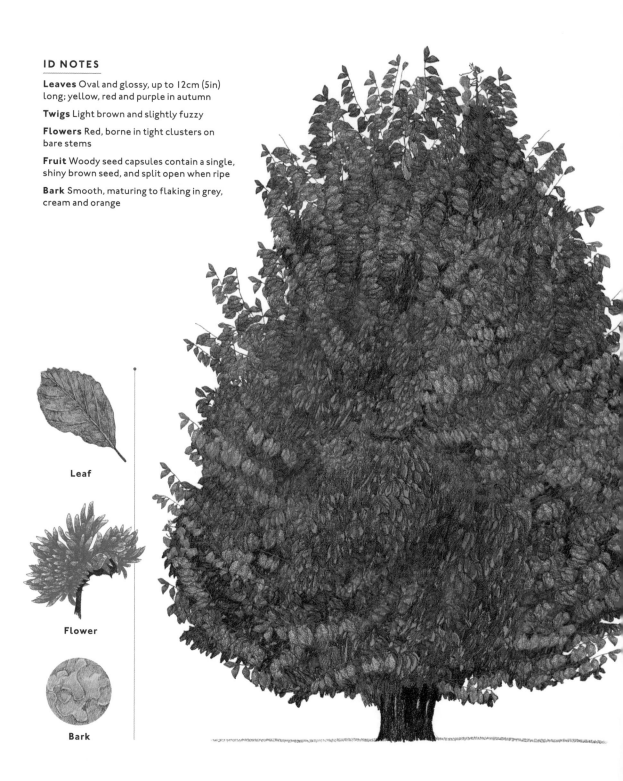

Leaf

Flower

Bark

TREE PROFILES

PERSIAN IRONWOOD

Parrotia persica

Famed for its autumn colour, the glossy, ribbed, mid-green leaves
of Persian ironwood turn incredible shades of yellow, orange,
red and purple in autumn. What's more, the tree holds onto
its leaves for longer than many other species, and so its
display can last for several weeks.

Following leaf fall, it's only another few weeks before Persian ironwood lights up again in late winter to spring, with tight clusters of red flowers that form dramatically on bare branches. The bark is attractive as well – silvery grey in colour, it starts to flake away as it matures, revealing young bark underneath in beautiful shades of pink, green and yellow.

Persian ironwood is native to Iran and the Caucasus, and is a member of the Hamamelidae (witch hazel) family. Its flowers bear similarities to witch hazel flowers. The cultivar 'Vanessa' is a more upright version than the species, making it more suitable for gardens. It will thrive in all soils but its autumn colour is best in slightly acidic soil.

CARE NOTES

Very little pruning is needed. Simply remove crossing and dead branches in late winter to early spring. Any reshaping or reducing of size should be done at this time, too.

Height/spread 8x8m (26x26ft) after 20 years

Life expectancy 150 years

Soil type Chalk, clay, loam, sand; acid, alkaline or neutral; moist but well-drained

Native to Northern Iran to the Caucasus

Hardiness H6

FRUIT
TREES

A fruit tree not only provides interest and wildlife value, but blossom and edible fruit, too. A mature apple or pear tree, for example, provides food and habitats for a huge range of species, as well as fruit for you to eat fresh and use in cooking. Fruit tree blossom is hugely important to early pollinators in spring. Many species can be trained as espalier or fan trees against a fence or wall (see p.151), helping the fruit to ripen, and making them excellent for small gardens. Leave windfalls for wildlife and don't worry about "pests" attacking the fruit. We all have to eat – simply cut around any tunnels or other signs of damage and look at ways you can increase predator numbers in your garden if the pests seem to be getting the upper hand.

PLUM

Prunus domestica

With their attractive blossom, fruit and wildlife value, plum trees make fantastic small garden trees.

Plums, gages and damsons are closely related. Plums are large and usually soft. Gages are smaller, round and sweet, while Mirabelle plums are smaller still, and range from yellow to dark pink. Damsons have a spicy, tart flavour and are used in cooking, particularly in jam. When buying, check the cultivar's pollination needs. Many are self-fertile, but others need another plum nearby to aid fertilisation. All can be fan-trained to save space (using a dwarfing rootstock, see pp.150–51). 'Victoria' is an all-round plum, self-fertile and crops well; 'Avalon' has large, red plums. Plum leaves are a foodplant for several moth species, the flowers are used by bees and the fruit eaten by birds, insects and small mammals.

Leaf

Twig

Flower

Height/spread 4x4m (13x13ft) after 20 years

Life expectancy 50 years

Soil type Clay, loam, sand; neutral; moist but well-drained

Native to Europe

Hardiness H5

ID NOTES

Leaves Dark green, oval, with small teeth and sometimes downy undersides

Twigs Dark brown, straight, sometimes spiny

Flowers White, with five petals, borne in clusters at the same time as the leaves form

Fruit/seed Large, fleshy fruit (drupe) with one large seed or stone

Bark Dark brown

CARE NOTES

Prune in summer to avoid silver leaf disease (see p.167), making an open bowl shape (see p.161). Mulch in autumn to suppress weeds and retain moisture.

APPLE

Malus domestica

Apple trees come in all shapes and sizes and make popular garden trees as
they're easy to grow and provide years of ornamental value and enjoyment.
The species *Malus domestica* is thought to have derived from the wild species
M. sieversii. Apples have been cultivated for thousands of years and there are
around 7,500 cultivated varieties.

Traditionally, apples grew to some 30m
(100ft) tall, but now most are grafted onto
rootstocks, which control their size and shape
(see pp.150–51). Apples can be grown as
standards (standalone trees with a single stem)
or trained as espaliers against a wall, fence or
wires (see p.151). There are more innovative
types, such as stepovers, which can be trained
as a low hedge, and "family" apple trees, with
several varieties grafted onto one rootstock.

For the best fruit crop, most apples need a
"pollination partner". This is a different type
of apple (or crab apple, pp.56–57) that flowers
at the same time and helps pollination. The
enormous variety of cultivars ranges from
commonly grown 'Cox's Orange Pippin'
and 'Spartan' to lesser-known 'Ashmead's
Kernel' and 'Claygate Pearmain'. Many
old apple varieties are linked to specific
geographical regions.

Apples are hugely beneficial to wildlife.
Their flowers provide food for pollinators
in spring, particularly types of mason bee.
Their bark and leaves are used by various
invertebrates, while windfalls are eaten
by birds, butterflies and small mammals.

CARE NOTES

Make sure you choose the right rootstock
for your purpose. Espaliers usually grow
on MM106 rootstock, while standards are
grown on M25.

Apples need regular pruning, particularly
if you're growing them as espaliers. Prune
standards in winter, removing crossing and
dead branches and helping to create an open,
bowl shape (see pp.160–61). Prune espaliers
in both summer and winter, cutting back
sideshoots to maintain the espalier shape
(see p.161).

Height/spread Up to 8x8m (26x26ft) after
20 years, depending on rootstock

Life expectancy 50–100 years

Soil type Clay, loam, sand; neutral; moist
but well-drained

Native to Central Asia

Hardiness H6

ID NOTES

Leaves Dark green, oval with serrated margins, variable length up to 7cm (3in)

Twigs Red/brown with short shoots and fuzzy leaf buds

Flowers Inflorescences of up to six, each with five petals, appearing in spring at the same time as the leaves unfurl

Fruit Edible apple with five chambers, each containing a number of seeds known as "pips"

Bark Red/grey speckled with white spots (lenticels), maturing to grey/brown and flaky

Leaf

Fruit

Flower

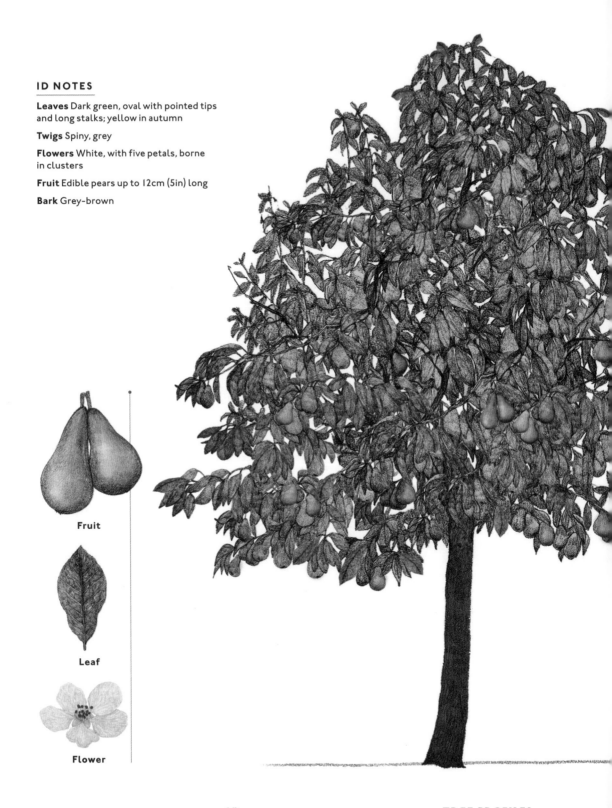

ID NOTES

Leaves Dark green, oval with pointed tips and long stalks; yellow in autumn

Twigs Spiny, grey

Flowers White, with five petals, borne in clusters

Fruit Edible pears up to 12cm (5in) long

Bark Grey-brown

Fruit

Leaf

Flower

PEAR

- -

Pyrus communis

Cultivated in Europe for thousands of years, pears come in many types and in a range of colours, shapes and sizes, ripening at different times. With their spring blossom and autumn fruit, they provide a long season of interest and are attractive to wildlife. There are also some ornamental pears that make excellent garden trees.

Like apples, pears are grown on different rootstocks to manage eventual shape and size (see pp.150–51). Pears are grown on quince rootstocks; Quince A or C are the most appropriate for a garden. They can also be trained as espalier trees against a fence or wall (see p.151). There's a huge variety of pears to choose from, with fruit ranging in colour from green to dark red. Like apples, most pears do best with a "pollination partner", which should be a different pear variety that flowers at the same time. If you have space for two pears then grow two, or check with neighbours to see if there are any growing locally.

Pears are also extremely valuable to wildlife. Bees and other insects use the blossom, while birds, small mammals and some insects eat the fruit. The leaves are used by moths, and other insects shelter in the bark of mature trees.

Weeping pear (*Pyrus salicifolia* 'Pendula') is a small, ornamental pear with silvery, willow-like foliage and cream-white flowers, then inedible green fruit. It's a useful tree for small gardens and copes well with pollution.

CARE NOTES

Prune pear trees in winter. First, remove crossing and dead branches, and aim for an open habit for standards (see pp.160–61). Prune espalier and fan-trained pears in summer and winter (see p.161). Pears are prone to leaf rust, visible as orange spots on the leaves in summer, and eventually cankers on the stems. The fungus relies on junipers to complete its lifecycle. Removing leaves can do more harm than good, but pruning out cankers in winter can help keep the problem under control.

Height/spread 12x8m (39x26ft) after 20 years on its own roots; 4x2m (13x6½ft) on a quince rootstock

Life expectancy 50–150 years

Soil type Clay, loam, sand; acid, alkaline or neutral; moist but well-drained

Native to Temperate regions of Europe, North Africa and Asia

Hardiness H6

CHERRY

Prunus spp.

This huge genus encompasses cherries grown mainly for their edible fruit as well
as other more ornamental cherries grown mainly for their blossom (see pp.38–39).
Cherries bear blossom in spring, fruit in autumn. and have glorious autumn
colour. They're great for wildlife too – open, single cherry flowers provide food
for bees, the fruit is eaten by birds (sorry – but it's good to share!) and the leaves
are nibbled by various invertebrate species.

Many fruiting cultivars have been bred
from the British native (*Prunus avium*),
and bird cherry (*P. padus*). All are grafted
onto rootstocks that make them smaller and
more manageable. Some cherries can be
fan-trained and grown against a wall or fence
to save space. Most are sweet to taste but the
sour cherry (*P. cerasus*) bears bitter-tasting
cherries on longer stalks. These cherries are
excellent in cooked dishes, such as cherry pie.

There's a huge variety of flowering cherries,
which make excellent garden trees. Many of
these are derived from Japanese species and
can be tall, dwarf, columnar or weeping in
habit. *P.* 'Amanogawa' is particularly small,
with flowers ranging from white to dark
pink. One flowering cherry, *P.* × *subhirtella*
'Autumnalis', flowers in autumn. Many have
striking bark, making them extra valuable in
winter. Bear in mind that, while flowering
cherries are very beautiful, only the single-
flowered species provide food for pollinators.
Cherries on ornamental trees have not been
bred for flavour and are not pleasant to eat.

CARE NOTES

Ornamental cherries don't need pruning,
unless it's to remove crossing or dead branches
(see pp.158–59). Prune edible cherries in
summer to avoid silver leaf disease (see p.167),
removing crossing and dead branches and
shaping the tree to have an open habit. Older
trees need little pruning – bear in mind that
sweet cherries fruit on wood that's at least
a year old, while sour cherries fruit on the
previous year's wood, so hard pruning will
result in no fruit for at least a year. Cherries
are prone to bacterial canker (see p166), visible
as leafless branches or branches with small
leaves, sunken bark, and distorted, swollen
or cracked patches.

Height/spread Up to 30m (100ft) after
20 years, but will vary due to cultivar
and rootstock

Life expectancy 60 years

Soil type Clay, loam, chalk, sand; acid,
alkaline or neutral; moist but well-drained

Native to Europe, Asia and parts of North Africa

Hardiness H6

TREE PROFILES

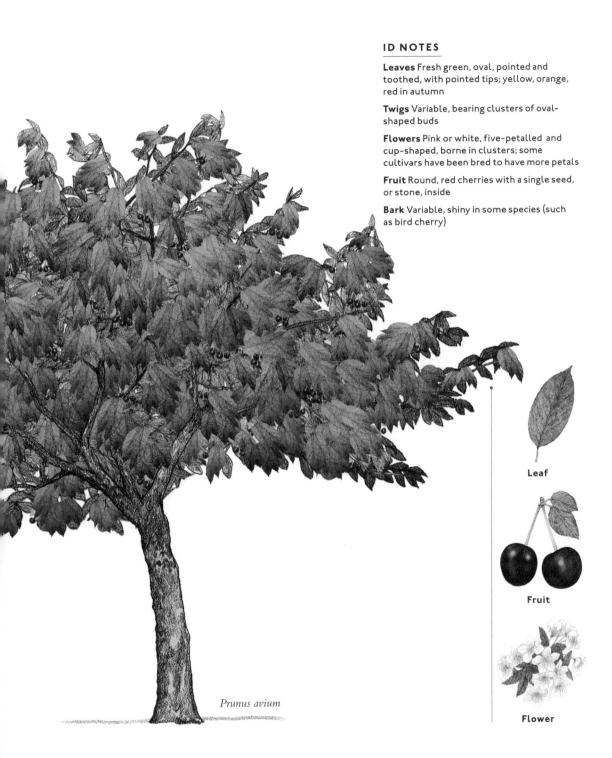

ID NOTES

Leaves Fresh green, oval, pointed and toothed, with pointed tips; yellow, orange, red in autumn

Twigs Variable, bearing clusters of oval-shaped buds

Flowers Pink or white, five-petalled and cup-shaped, borne in clusters; some cultivars have been bred to have more petals

Fruit Round, red cherries with a single seed, or stone, inside

Bark Variable, shiny in some species (such as bird cherry)

Prunus avium

Leaf

Fruit

Flower

ID NOTES

Leaves 16cm (6¼in) long and 3cm (1¼in) wide, lanceolate (wider in the middle) in shape; golden/red in autumn

Twigs New growth is green/red, fading to brown/grey; leaf buds are blunt

Flowers Pink, five-petalled, 2–3cm (¾–1¼in) diameter, appearing on bare stems

Fruit Flesh surrounding a hard seed (drupe). Fuzzy, hair-coated fruits are known as peaches and smooth fruits as nectarines

Bark Dark grey, smooth when young, maturing to scaly

Fruit

Twig

Flower

TREE PROFILES

PEACH

Prunus persica

Providing ornamental value from spring to autumn, as well as delicious fruit,
peach trees are perfect for small gardens. Growing to no more than 4m (13ft) in
height and with an average life expectancy of up to 20 years, they're a good choice
if you want to plant something short-term – there's no risk of regretting your
planting decisions 50 years later.

Despite being fully hardy, peach trees flower early in the year, which puts the flowers (and the resulting fruits) at risk of frost damage. If you want a reliable source of peaches (or nectarines) you'll need to grow them in a sheltered spot. In Britain, most peach trees are fan-trained (see p.151) and planted against a south-facing wall that retains heat from the day, preventing overnight frost from destroying the flowers. They're also a good option for growing in containers.

The *persica* part of the peach's species name refers to Persia (Iran), where peaches have been cultivated for thousands of years. However, peaches originate in China.

Peach blossom is valuable to pollinators but, as it appears so early, only a few species get to see it. To ensure fertilisation, it may be best to hand-pollinate peaches, by gently passing a small paintbrush over each flower.

Nectarines are closely related to peaches and have the same growing requirements and nutritional values, but lack the fuzzy peach skin. It's said that peaches are more suitable for baking as the cooking process softens them, while nectarines remain firm.

CARE NOTES

Protect early flowers with two or three layers of horticultural fleece, which you simply drape over the tree to stop frost reaching the blossom. This needs to be removed during the day. Peaches are prone to the fungal disease peach leaf curl, which distorts leaves and causes them to fall prematurely, resulting in a loss of vigour. As the spores are spread by rain splash, erecting a lean-to rain shelter with plastic sheeting can help stop the spread of the disease. Alternatively, grow your peach tree in a greenhouse or other sheltered environment, or choose a variety that shows some resistance to peach leaf curl.

Height/spread 4x4m (13x13ft) after 20 years

Life expectancy 20 years

Soil type Chalk, loam, sand; acid, alkaline or neutral; moist but well-drained

Native to China

Hardiness H4

FIG

Ficus carica

Hailing from the Mediterranean, figs can be grown in cooler climates but need
a bit of help. They do best in a very sheltered spot such as against a wall, away
from prevailing wind, and they need well-drained soil. As well as providing fruit,
figs are highly ornamental, with gorgeous grey bark and large, pale green
three- to five-lobed leaves.

Fig trees can be fan-trained to grow flat against a sunny wall and also work well in pots – in fact they seem to produce more fruit when their roots are slightly constricted. If you grow figs in the ground, constrict their growing space by burying vertical panel, such as corrugated iron or flagstones, around the rootball.

While most fig trees are hardy, some have been developed especially for a British climate. The cultivars 'Brown Turkey' and 'Brunswick' are particularly suitable. Figs can be dioecious – having both male and female

flowers – which are unusually held within the fruit. However, fig cultivars available in Britain don't need pollination to fruit. Ripe figs are loved by blackbirds and some insects.

Some fig varieties outside the UK rely on a small chalcid wasp to pollinate the flowers, which are inside the fruit. The female crawls into the fruit and lays her eggs, and then her offspring grow within the flower, mate and chew their way out. The wasps can become trapped and die, and the carnivorous fig fruit releases enzymes to break down the wasps' bodies and feed on them.

CARE NOTES

Transplant figs in pots every couple of years to a slightly larger pot – not too large as figs do best with a smaller root run. Protect from harsh frost with horticultural fleece – smaller trees can be wrapped in a drawstring bag made of fleece. For fan-trained or large trees, drape over a couple of layers of fleece. After autumn harvesting, you will be left with two types of figs – tiny pea-sized "embryo" fruit and larger, unripe figs. Remove the larger figs as they will not ripen and will take energy away from the smaller fruits that will ripen the following year.

Height/spread 4x4m (13x13ft) after 20 years

Life expectancy 200 years

Soil type Chalk, loam, sand; alkaline or
neutral; moist but well-drained

Native to Southern Europe, Asia

Hardiness H4

Leaves Large, leathery and bright green with three to five lobes; yellow in autumn

Twigs Olive-green with pointed leaf buds

Flowers Small and inconspicuous

Fruit Technically a bulbous stem containing clusters of seeds within

Bark Grey-brown, smooth

Leaf

Twig

Fruit

Flower

CITRUS

Citrus **spp.**

Oranges and lemons, along with limes and kumquats, are all part of the highly ornamental *Citrus* genus.

Citrus trees make fine garden plants in warmer areas, and with climate change may thrive outdoors all year. However, it's currently best to grow them in pots that you can move indoors for winter. The fragrant flowers appear all year but are most prevalent in late winter. The fruit takes a year to mature so flowers and fruit are often visible at the same time. Oranges tolerate a minimum winter night temperature of 10°C (50°F). Kumquats tolerate down to 7°C (45°F). The easiest, and hardiest, are lemons and Seville oranges. Limes need warmer temperatures than most British gardens offer.

Citrus × *limon*

ID NOTES

Leaves Glossy, oval, fresh green

Twigs Green, fading to brown

Flowers Extremely fragrant, five-petalled, white

Fruit Citrus fruits are edible specialised berries, known as hesperidiums; they vary in shape, colour and size but all have a peelable rind, known as a pericarp

Bark Dark brown

CARE NOTES

Citrus trees are hungry feeders so need regular feeding with a proprietary citrus food. They can be prone to pests such as mealy bug and red spider mite, especially if grown in a conservatory or greenhouse.

Leaf

Twig

Flower

Height/spread Variable, up to 20m (66ft) after 20 years, but often smaller; about 1.5m (5ft) in a pot

Life expectancy 50 years

Soil type Chalk, loam, sand; alkaline or neutral; moist but well-drained

Native to Asia and Australia

Hardiness H2

TREE PROFILES

MULBERRY

Morus nigra

Slow-growing, the mulberry can take seven years to start to produce, but will then provide you with masses of delicious, sharp-tasting fruits for many years.

The fruits can be used in place of blackberries and raspberries in many recipes, including tarts and fools. They make an excellent jam, but are best eaten fresh with cream and sugar. Mulberries are excellent for wildlife – which means you'll have to share the fruit with blackbirds.

Mulberries are used in traditional Chinese medicines, where they are known as sang shen. They are a good source of iron and vitamin C. Plant compounds in mulberries have been linked to lower cholesterol and blood sugar, and reducing the risk of cancer.

ID NOTES

Leaves Heart-shaped with downy undersides and faint toothed edges; yellow in autumn

Twigs Thin and bendy with rounded, red-brown leaf buds

Flowers Insignificant and green

Fruit Blackberry-like with a sharp, acidic taste

Bark Grey-brown, rough and grooved

CARE NOTES

Stake the mulberry when planting (see pp.148–49). Prune in winter to prevent sap bleeding from the cuts, removing crossing, crowded or damaged shoots (see pp.158–59).

Leaf

Flower

Fruit

Height/spread 12x8m (39x26ft) after 20 years

Life expectancy 100 years

Soil type Chalk, clay, loam, sand; acid, alkaline or neutral; moist but well-drained

Native to Southwest Asia

Hardiness H6

BERRYING
TREES

Unsurprisingly, berrying trees are those that produce berries.
While most aren't edible for humans, they are extremely
valuable to wildlife, particularly birds. Some berries have
extremely high levels of antioxidants, which help reduce the
physical stresses of winter migration. Planting a berrying tree
in your garden will provide an annual source of antioxidant-
rich food for wildlife, and lots of colour and interest for you
too! While some berrying trees, like holly, have inconspicuous
flowers, others such as elder have beautiful flowers, giving
them a long season of interest. Many are also suitable
for hedging plants.

ELDER

Sambucus nigra

A versatile plant with high wildlife value, elder can be grown as a tree, shrub, or in a hedge.

Left unpruned, elder grows into a tall tree. In gardens, it can be cut back to keep it small, resulting in larger, more ornamental leaves (but sacrificing flowers and fruit). Its leaves are a caterpillar foodplant of many moth species, its flowers are loved by pollinators, and its berries eaten by birds. Insects hibernate in the crevices of its mature bark. The flowers can be used to make elderflower cordial or wine, and the berries in jams, sauces and other summer recipes. The berries have high levels of vitamin C. *Sambucus nigra* f. *porphyrophylla* 'Eva' (or 'Black Lace') has finely cut, almost black leaves, pink-flushed blooms, red-black berries, and red autumn leaves.

ID NOTES

Leaves Fresh green, pinnate with five to seven leaflets; red in autumn in some species

Twigs Green, with an unpleasant smell

Flowers Flat umbels of cream, highly scented florets

Fruit/seed Purple-black berries borne in clusters

Bark Corky with deep crevices

CARE NOTES

Little routine care is needed. To keep your elder as a small shrub with larger leaves, prune it back annually, when dormant to around 50cm (20in) above the ground – never prune beyond the point where the shrub starts to branch.

Leaf

Berries

Flower

Height/spread 8x4m (26x13ft) after 20 years

Life expectancy 60 years

Soil type Chalk, clay, loam, sand; acid, alkaline or neutral; moist but well-drained

Native to Europe, North Africa, southwest Asia

Hardiness H6

ID NOTES

Leaves Glossy, dark green and oval; spiky when younger

Twigs Grey and fuzzy with blunt leaf buds

Flowers Inconspicuous, white with four petals

Fruit/seed Small red berries

Bark Smooth with "warts" or markings

Leaf

Twig and berries

Flower

TREE PROFILES

ENGLISH HOLLY

Ilex aquifolium

English holly is one of many species of holly across the world. It's a versatile evergreen shrub or small tree – grow it as a shrub or as part of a hedge, or train it as a standard tree with a lollipop shape. Long used to decorate homes in winter, holly is associated with fertility. In traditional folklore it's considered bad luck to cut down a holly tree.

English holly, along with other holly species, has excellent wildlife value. Its dense, prickly habit makes it a source of shelter for garden birds, its flowers are visited by bees and other pollinators, and its berries are eaten by birds and small mammals. Several butterfly and moth species, notably the holly blue butterfly, use holly as a caterpillar foodplant. Fallen leaves allowed to accumulate beneath a holly hedge may be used by hedgehogs and other overwintering animals. Male and female flowers appear on different plants. When buying holly, make sure you have a female plant, as it's only the female plants that bear berries. A male holly will be needed nearby to ensure pollination.

As well as the standard English holly, there are plenty of cultivars, some with different coloured berries and/or variegated foliage. Some of the most appealing are *Ilex × altaclerensis* 'Golden King', which has grey-green leaves with a golden yellow margin and bright red berries, and *I. aquifolium* 'Bacciflava', which has yellow berries.

CARE NOTES

Holly needs very little care after planting, but keep it well watered for the first two years or so to help it establish. Pruning is just a matter of trimming to size in late winter or early spring – simply cut back those growing as a hedge or shrubs to keep them to the desired shape. Remove lower branches of standard trees to maintain a clear trunk.

Height/spread 12x8m (39x26ft) after 20 years

Life expectancy 7 years, although some can live for up to 300 years

Soil type Chalk, clay, loam, sand; acid, alkaline or neutral; moist but well-drained

Native to Western and southern Europe, northwest Africa, southwest Asia

Hardiness H6

ROWAN

Sorbus aucuparia

A fantastic tree, the rowan, or mountain ash, is typically associated
with high altitudes (as "mountain ash" suggests). Its leaves resemble those
of the ash tree, but that's where the similarities end. It makes an excellent
garden tree, being compact, excellent for wildlife, and providing
a long season of interest. Rowan trees can cope well with pollution,
and so are a good choice for urban areas.

From late spring, the rowan is covered in creamy blossom, while in autumn it bears fantastic bright red berries, although these don't last long as the birds enjoy them so much. Vivd autumn leaves add a final burst of colour before the leaves fall. Traditionally grown to ward against witches, rowans are now a popular tree to grow for wildlife.

There are many *Sorbus* species across the northern hemisphere, including some closely related rowans, plus whitebeams and service trees. Many have been hybridised and some wonderful cultivars have resulted from them. *S.* 'Joseph Rock' is thought to be a natural hybrid – a botanist and explorer named Joseph Rock sent fruit and seeds from China to Edinburgh early in the 20th century, and a beautiful yellow-berried sorbus grew from one, although its heritage is unknown. As well as beautiful yellow berries, this cultivar also boasts incredible autumn leaf colour. All 'Joseph Rock' rowans are grafted onto other rowan trees (see p.150) as they do not come true from seed.

CARE NOTES

Rowan trees are generally healthy and need little care. Remove dead and crossing stems as and when you need to (see pp.158–59), and water in very dry conditions. Grafted cultivars will produce suckers, which are new stems growing from the rootstock. Remove these when they're young, either by rubbing them off by hand when they are buds, or trimming them back to the ground or stump if they are older.

Height/spread 12x8m (39x26ft) after 20 years

Life expectancy 100 years

Soil type Loam, sand; acid, neutral; moist but well-drained

Native to Europe, Asia

Hardiness H6

TREE PROFILES

ID NOTES

Leaves Pinnate, with up to eight pairs of leaflets, plus a "terminal" leaflet at the end, each leaflet long, oval and toothed; yellow in autumn

Twigs Hairy, becoming smooth with age; leaf buds are large and purple, and look like fat mittens

Flowers Five-petalled, cream, carried in dense clusters

Fruit/seed Dense clusters of bright red berries

Bark Smooth and silver-grey

Leaf

Twig

Flower

Berrying trees

HAWTHORN

Crataegus monogyna

One of the best garden trees, hawthorn is compact and interesting to look at. It's an absolute magnet for wildlife – its leaves are a caterpillar foodplant for many species of moth, its flowers are visited by pollinating bees and flies, its berries are eaten by birds, and its gnarled, mature bark has crevices for hibernating insects. Mature trees provide nesting spots for birds, while a hawthorn hedge offers nesting opportunities for small mammals, too.

There are many species of hawthorn from various regions in the northern hemisphere. A number of cultivars have been bred from these, and you'll find double-flowered specimens that produce an even more impressive spring display. *Crataegus persimilis* 'Prunifolia' is more compact than *C. monogyna*, and has more dramatic autumn colour. In the British Isles, as well as *C. monogyna*, there's also *C. laevigata*, or the Midland hawthorn, which flowers earlier and has slightly looser-lobed leaves.

Hawthorn has long been associated with the month of May, which it's sometimes named after. Its flowers have an unusual smell – in the Middle Ages the flowers were said to smell of the Plague, and it was considered bad luck to bring hawthorn flowers into the home. Recent research has found that hawthorn flowers contain trimethylamine, a chemical also found in newly deceased bodies. The flowers really do, therefore, smell of the dead – presumably to attract insect pollinators, such as flies, to fertilise the blossom.

CARE NOTES

Hawthorns need very little care. Water well in the first two years after planting and trim shrubs and hedging plants into shape in autumn. Remove crossing and dead branches from trees (see pp.158–59),and cut away lower branches from time to time when the tree is dormant to maintain a clear trunk.

Height/spread 8x8m (26x26ft) after 20 years

Life expectancy 150 years

Soil type Chalk, clay, loam, sand; acid, alkaline or neutral; moist but well-drained

Native to Europe, North Africa, southwest Asia

Hardiness H7

ID NOTES

Leaves Small, fresh green, deeply lobed; yellow in autumn

Twigs Slender, brown and thorny

Flowers Strongly fragrant, five-petalled, white and borne in clusters

Fruit/seed Red berries, known as haws

Bark Grey brown, maturing to develop fissures

Leaf

Berries

Twig

Flower

FLOWERING
TREES

All trees flower, but some trees' flowers are bigger and better than others, making them a perfect choice for a garden. Here I've picked a selection with particularly lovely flowers, often without subsequent berries or fruit – but if you're after flowers and fruit, you'll also find beautiful flowering trees in the Fruit trees section (see pp.64–77). When buying flowering trees, it's worth checking to make sure they're suitable for pollinators. Sadly, not all flowering trees are – the flowers may be "double" (having extra petals at the expense of accessible pollen and nectar) or, if they're native to another country or region of the world, they could have the wrong shape for native pollinator mouths. Unless stated, all trees listed in this section have some value for pollinators.

Leaf

Seed capsule

CRAPE MYRTLE

Lagerstroemia indica

Flowering from late summer to autumn, crape myrtles bear frilly flowers, like crêpe paper, in a range of colours, from pink and red to white.

Crape myrtle can be grown as a small tree or shrub, reaching 8m (26ft), but half that size is more likely in cooler climates. Insects love the flowers. A stalwart of North American and southern European city planting schemes, crape myrtles are rarely grown in the UK as they are hardy only to -5°C (23°F) and don't reliably flower. That said, with climate change and a south-facing wall, you could consider growing one, as they put on quite a show. They can be grown in pots and moved indoors in winter, depending on size.

ID NOTES

Leaves Long, dark green, tinged with bronze when young; red, golden, orange in autumn

Twigs Straight, red-brown, with small leaf buds

Flowers Crêpe-like, conical panicles in a range of colours

Fruit Clusters of upright seed capsules that remain throughout winter

Bark Peeling, grey-brown

CARE NOTES

Crape myrtles flower on the current season's growth, so annual hard pruning in winter promotes the best display. Simply cut the current season's growth back by half, and remove suckers at the base on standard trees (but leave them for those grown as shrubs).

Height/spread 8x8m (26x26ft) after 20 years

Life expectancy 50 years

Soil type Chalk, loam, sand; acid, alkaline or neutral; well-drained

Native to China, Korea

Hardiness H3

MAGNOLIA

Magnolia **spp.**

Iconic spring-flowering small trees or shrubs, magnolias bear tulip- or star-shaped flowers in pink or white, many with a strong fragrance. They can be deciduous or evergreen, and the different species range in size from 2m (6½ft) to 15m (49ft) high. The flowers of deciduous magnolias often appear before the leaves, making their spring display especially dramatic.

There's a magnolia for every garden, and it's worth spending time choosing the right one, as they're very slow growing. Most require acid to neutral soil, but some will tolerate more alkaline soils, especially if it's enriched with an annual dressing of compost or manure. These include *Magnolia grandiflora*, *M. delavayi*, *M. kobus*, *M.* × *loebneri*, *M. stellata* and *M. wilsonii*. Some smaller varieties, such as *M. stellata* 'Royal Star', *M. denudata* 'Sunrise' and *M.* 'George Henry Kern', can be grown in pots.

Always grow magnolias in a sheltered spot so frost doesn't spoil the look of the flowers.

M. stellata 'Jane Platt' is one of the best magnolias for a small garden, growing to an eventual height of just 3m (10ft). *M. grandiflora* is evergreen, offering year-round interest, but grows much taller so is best for a larger space.

Magnolias have been around for millennia, since before bees, and so their flowers are pollinated by beetles. A variety of beetles, including pollen beetles, will visit and pollinate magnolia flowers, and while bees are still attracted to the pollen the flowers have on offer, they don't have a role in the fertilisation of the flowers.

CARE NOTES

Magnolias do best in a rich soil so mulch annually in spring, with well-rotted manure or compost. They need little pruning, but if you want to shape yours or remove dead or damaged material (see pp.159–60), prune deciduous varieties from summer to autumn, and evergreen types in summer.

Height/spread From 2x3m (6½x10ft) to 15x10m (49x33ft) after 20 years

Life expectancy 100 years

Soil type Clay, loam, sand; acid, neutral; moist but well-drained

Native to Asia, the Americas and West Indies

Hardiness H6

ID NOTES

Leaves Variable, typically green-golden, large and oval; golden yellow in autumn in deciduous varieties

Twigs Brown, bendy with fat buds

Flowers Goblet- or star-shaped

Fruit/seed Clusters of fleshy fruit

Bark Brown and smooth

Leaf

Twig

Flower

ID NOTES

Leaves Oval, green, with prominent veining; some species have orange, red or purple autumn leaves

Twigs Slender, with opposite buds; brightly coloured in some species

Flowers Variable; from clusters of small, inconspicuous flowers to large flower-like bracts

Fruit/seed Small, dark berries, elongated hip-like fruit or rounded, bumpy fruit

Bark Smooth and grey, ageing to mottled and bumpy or peeling; or reddish, ageing to mottled

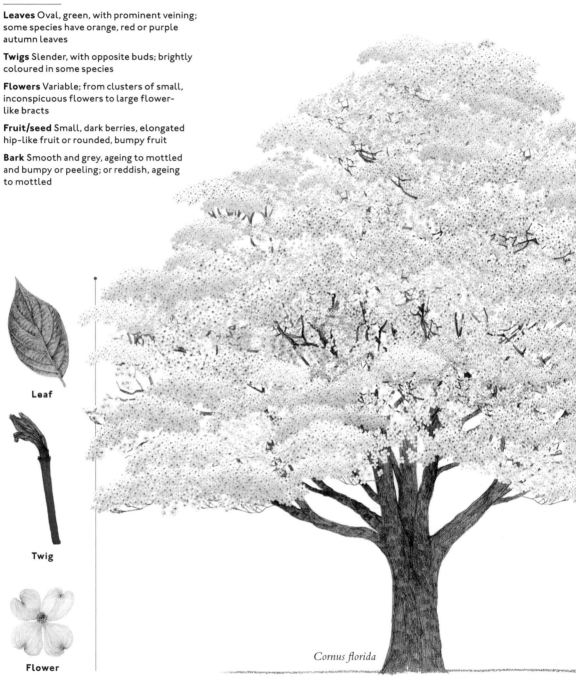

Leaf

Twig

Flower

Cornus florida

TREE PROFILES

DOGWOOD

Cornus **spp.**

The *Cornus* genus is a varied group of up to 60 species, and this diversity
means there's one for your garden. Flowering dogwoods, including
C. florida and *C. kousa,* are highly ornamental shrubs or small trees, grown
for their colourful late-spring bracts (modified leaves that are larger and more
spectacular than the flowers). Shrubby dogwoods, including the British native
C. sanguinea, are grown for their colourful winter stems.

Flowering dogwoods are grown for their ornamental value over everything else. These include beautiful *C. kousa* 'Miss Satomi', a pink-flowered dogwood, bearing masses of blooms in midsummer, and *C. florida,* which has huge, petal-like white bracts before its leaves unfurl, and glorious autumn colour.

Want to grow a tree for wildlife? Choose *C. sanguinea* and leave it to grow into a hedge or small tree. If you wish to prune it hard to produce colourful winter colour (see care notes, below), this will be at the expense of shrubby habitat, which many wild species need for shelter.

C. mas is a fantastic tree for small gardens as it holds interest over a long season. From late winter, its bare branches are covered in clusters of small, bright yellow flowers, which are followed by cherry-like fruit (edible to people but also loved by birds). Its green leaves turn shades of yellow, red and purple in autumn.

CARE NOTES

Shrubby dogwoods (including *C. sanguinea*) do best in moist soil. For colourful winter stems, cut them to the ground in early spring, and the new growth stimulated by the pruning will be much brighter the following winter. Flowering dogwoods do much better in fertile, neutral to acidic soil and need very little pruning. Mulch all types annually, in spring or autumn.

Height/spread Varied, 3–8m (10–26ft), but most are pruned to keep growth in check

----

Life expectancy 70 years (flowering dogwoods); 80–100 years (shrubby dogwoods)

Soil type Chalk, clay, loam, sand; acid, alkaline or neutral; moist but well-drained

----

Native to North America, parts of Europe, China and Japan

Hardiness H4–H6

LILAC

Syringa vulgaris

Popular in gardens, lilacs can be grown either as a shrub or a multi-stemmed small tree. They have extremely fragrant, star-shaped flowers, set off beautifully by fresh green leaves. It's thought that the colour lilac was named after the shade of purple of the tree's flowers, although the flowers of some varieties actually come in a range of colours, including pink, purple, yellow and white – not just lilac!

Lilac trees are particularly good for small gardens as their flowers have a lovely fragrance and they're compact so they'll never outgrow their space. They can be grown as multi-stemmed shrubs, or you can remove some of the lower branches to make more of a standard tree shape.

One of the best garden lilacs is *Syringa vulgaris* 'Sensation'. This bears masses of rich purple flowers with a cream margin, and a strong fragrance, filling the air with scent. *S. vulgaris* 'Andenken an Ludwig Späth' has pink-purple flowers. "French lilac" trees are double-flowered cultivars that were bred by the French breeder Victor Lemoine in the nineteenth century.

Lilacs have been naturalised across North America and parts of Europe, but are truly native to the rocky mountains of the Balkans.

CARE NOTES

Prune young plants to create an open framework and remove dead, crossing or too-long branches (see pp.158–59). Very little pruning is needed on established trees, and be careful if you do as lilacs flower on the previous year's wood, so you risk losing some flowers; late spring after flowering is the best time to prune.

Height/spread 4x4m (13x13ft) after 20 years

Life expectancy 50 years

Soil type Chalk, clay, loam, sand; acid, alkaline, neutral; moist but well-drained

Native to Southeast Europe

Hardiness H6

ID NOTES

Leaves Heart-shaped, fresh green and smooth, with prominent veining; green in autumn

Twigs Brown with green leaf buds that turn purple in winter

Flowers Purple, star-shaped, in dense panicles with a strong fragrance

Fruit/seed Brown seed capsules

Bark Grey-brown, smooth when young, maturing to flaky

Leaf

Twig

Seed capsule

Flowering trees

EVERGREEN
TREES

Evergreen trees are useful in small gardens as they provide
winter interest when other trees are dormant and leafless.
But it's not just in winter that evergreens stand out – many
have beautiful flowers and fruit at other times of the year,
while others provide a solid green backdrop for more
colourful plants. You'll have noticed a few evergreen trees
in other sections, but here's a good selection of trees
renowned for their evergreen beauty.

MEDITERRANEAN CYPRESS

Cupressus sempervirens

Popular with garden designers, the Mediterranean (or Italian or Tuscan) cypress is an elegant conifer that grows tall and slender.

In a large garden, grow cypress trees in a row where they can form an impressive backdrop to the rest of your garden, which you can then balance with more rounded shapes. A row can be used to line an entrance or mark a boundary, or to make a sophisticated architectural statement. In a small garden, just one or two trees can provide an evergreen "accent" to a border or gravel garden. Choose a sunny, sheltered site with well-drained soil. In the Mediterranean, this evergreen is known as the "drama tree" because it has a tendency to bend at the slightest breeze.

Height/spread 12x4m (39x13ft) after 20–50 years

Life expectancy 500 years

Soil type Chalk, clay, loam, sand; acid, alkaline or neutral; well-drained

Native to Mediterranean

Hardiness H5

Bark

Cone

Leaf

ID NOTES

Leaves Dense sprays of grey-green foliage

Twigs Red-brown

Cones Small, 2–3cm (¾–1¼in) in diameter

Bark Red-brown with vertical ridges, ageing to grey

CARE NOTES

No pruning is required, but you may want to remove the odd branch growing in the wrong direction. Brown patches may be caused by cypress aphid (*Cinara cupressivora*), found in summer, or Coryneum canker, caused by a fungus and resulting in branch dieback. Most brown patches will heal naturally, while branch dieback can be pruned out. Encourage birds into your garden to keep aphids at bay.

WILD PRIVET

Ligustrum vulgare

A semi-evergreen shrub, occasionally forming a multi-branched tree, wild privet has spectacular summer flowers. It's commonly found in hedgerows and on the edges of woodland, as well as scrubby grassland. In gardens it makes an excellent hedging plant, although has a slightly wilder growing habit than the more commonly used garden privet (*Ligustrum ovalifolium*).

Sadly, wild privet is usually trimmed before the creamy-white flowers emerge, especially when it's part of a hedge, but if you leave them to grow you'll be rewarded with masses of bees, as privet flowers are a bee magnet. These flowers are followed by small, dark berries, which are poisonous to humans but popular with a number of garden birds. It's the main foodplant of the privet hawk moth, as well as a few other moth species, and provides shelter for small birds and mammals.

Privet will grow almost anywhere, and can cope with sea winds, full sun, partial shade, and light, dry soil as well as sandy conditions. The only thing it doesn't do well in is boggy soil.

CARE NOTES

Keep young plants watered and weed-free for two years after planting. Prune hedges annually (see pp.158–60), ideally in winter after berrying so that the bees and birds can make the most of its flowers and fruit. By this time of year there will be no danger of disturbing nesting birds either. Stunted growth and yellow leaves are a sign of boggy soil, and efforts should be made to improve drainage, such as digging around the plants and adding gravel.

Height/spread 4x4m (13x13ft), but is usually clipped as a hedge

Life expectancy 50 years

Soil type Chalk, clay, loam, sand; acid, alkaline or neutral; moist but well-drained

Native to Europe, including the British Isles

Hardiness H6

ID NOTES

Leaves Oval, glossy and dark green with a central rib

Twigs Grey-brown with alternate buds

Flower Cream, lilac-like panicles

Fruit/seed Small black, poisonous berries

Bark Grey-brown and smooth

Flower

Fruit

Evergreen trees

ID NOTES

Leaves Oblong, glossy and green with a paler central rib

Twigs Red-brown, smooth

Flowers Urn-shaped, white with a pink flush

Fruit/seed Round, strawberry-like

Bark Rusty brown and peeling

Leaf

Fruit

Flower

STRAWBERRY TREE

Arbutus unedo

The strawberry tree bears delicate, urn-shaped flowers and at the same time strawberry-like fruit, giving it the common name of strawberry tree. All these features make it a beautiful choice for a garden tree. Its evergreen, bay-like leaves take the strawberry tree's ornamental value through into winter.

A magnificent sight, the strawberry tree is native to the Mediterranean where it grows among cork trees and craggy hilltops in the driest soils. It's also native to Ireland, but not the rest of the British Isles. Hardy down to -10°C (14°F), it can be grown in most regions of the UK.

Tolerant of pollution and salt, the strawberry tree thrives both in cities and coastal gardens. It doesn't grow too big, so it makes an excellent choice for a small garden. Its urn-shaped flowers are popular with bees and its fruit is loved by birds (the fruit is also edible for humans, but not particularly tasty).

The variety 'Compacta' grows to a maximum height and spread of just 2.5m (8ft) and is suitable for growing in a pot.

CARE NOTES

Young plants may need protection from hard frosts – simply drape with a couple of layers of horticultural fleece or move pot-grown plants under cover. Cold winds can cause leaf scorch. Fungal leaf spot disease can affect strawberry trees. This disease is usually nothing to worry about but can cause leaf drop and loss of vigour. Remove and burn infected leaves. Avoid pruning, unless it's to remove damaged or crossing stems. Mulch in autumn.

Height/spread 8x8m (26x26ft) after 20 years

Life expectancy 400 years

Soil type Loam, sand; acid, alkaline or neutral; moist but well-drained

Native to Mediterranean, northwest Europe and Ireland

Hardiness H5

SEED- AND NUT-BEARING TREES

Seeds and nuts are invaluable to wildlife, and many are edible for people, too. Plant a seed- or nut-bearing tree and the wildlife will visit your garden for years. Squirrels and large birds such as woodpeckers may come looking for acorns and pine cones, while smaller birds such as blue tits will hang upside down from the slimmest of branches to pick at dangling seeds from silver birch and alder. Bear in mind that any seeds and nuts that fall to the ground will try to germinate. Squirrels, too, will bury the seeds and forget about them, resulting in free tree seedlings for you and your neighbours!

TREE PROFILES

SPINDLE

Euonymus europaeus

In autumn spindle's leaves turn glorious shades of red and orange, before falling to reveal pink fruits with bright orange seeds, which persist into winter.

A small tree, spindle can reach 9m (30ft), but is more likely to reach about 4m (13ft). As a British native, it's a great option for attracting wildlife – its flowers are pollinated by insects and its seeds eaten by birds. The leaves feed caterpillars of several moth species, including the magpie, spindle ermine and scorched moths, as well as the holly blue butterfly. Aphids flock to spindle leaves in spring and summer, providing birds with a much-needed source of natural food. Be careful around children and pets – all parts of spindle can cause discomfort if ingested. Wear gloves, and wash hands after touching it.

Leaf

Twig

Seeds

Height/spread 9x4m (30x13ft) after 10–20 years

Life expectancy 150 years

Soil type Chalk, clay, loam, sand; acid, alkaline or neutral; moist but well-drained

Native to Europe, Asia

Hardiness H6

ID NOTES

Leaves Oval, fresh green; red and orange in autumn

Twigs Deep green when young, thin and straight

Flowers Small white/yellow, in panicles

Fruit/seed Pink fruit cases that split to reveal bright orange seeds

Bark Deep green, fading to brown and developing corky fissures with age

CARE NOTES

Spindle is relatively trouble free. There's no need to prune unless you want to reduce its size. If you do need to prune, do so in spring or autumn. Avoid waterlogged areas.

ID NOTES

Leaves Rounded, fresh green and never pointed; orange and yellow in autumn

Twigs Spotted with an orange/red tip; sticky

Flowers Cone-like female catkins and tassel-like male catkins

Fruit/seed Borne in tiny brown female catkins that look like cones and stay on the tree throughout winter

Bark Dark, fissured

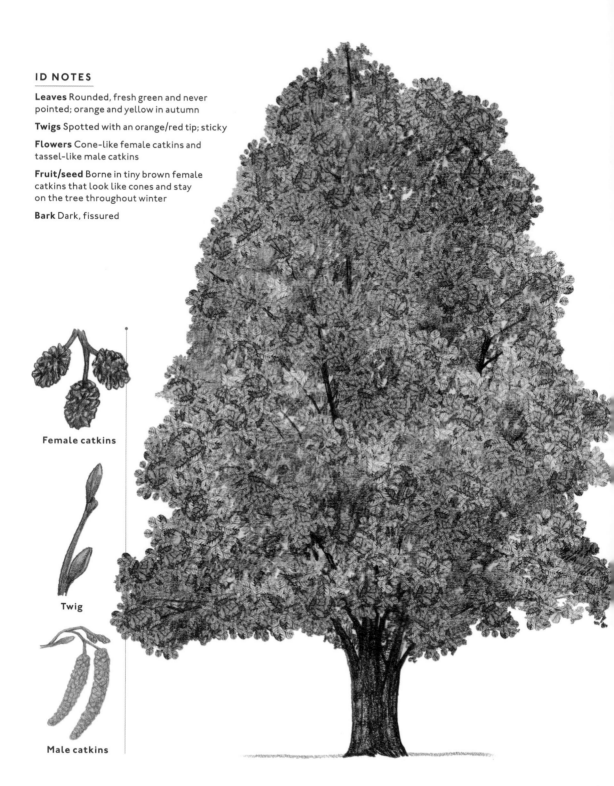

Female catkins

Twig

Male catkins

ALDER

Alnus glutinosa

Strongly associated with wetter habitats, the alder is a wonderful British native tree that's often found in wet woodland or "carrs" with other moisture-tolerant trees, such as silver birch. It has a conical shape and gently rustling leaves, making it a fine choice for a large garden. Alder can also be grown as a hedge, and is particularly useful for waterlogged or boggy gardens.

Alder is the foodplant for several moth caterpillars, including the wonderfully named alder kitten. In spring, its male catkins offer early pollen for bees. However, they are actually wind-pollinated and, once pollinated, the female catkins grow woody and resemble tiny pine cones. These open in autumn to release their flat, waxy seeds, which have two corky wings to help them float on water and disperse to new ground. The remaining seeds are eaten by siskins, redpolls and goldfinches – alder seed is the main source of winter food for the siskin, which extracts it by reaching far into the crevices of the catkin with its long, slim bill.

Below ground it has a strong relationship with the bacterium *Frankia alni*, which forms nodules on its roots. The nodules absorb nitrogen from the air, making it available to the tree. In return, the alder provides the bacteria with carbon. This enables the alder to grow on poor soils, and improves the soil.

When cut, alder wood turns bright orange. Alder trees have long been regarded with suspicion, and in Ireland it was considered bad luck to pass an alder.

CARE NOTES

Alder needs moist soil to thrive. Pruning is rarely necessary although you may want to remove crossing or dead stems (see pp.158–59) in late spring to summer. Alder is prone to alder sucker, a sap-sucking bug with nymphs that are covered in white, waxy threads. These can be quite noticeable but rarely cause damage to the tree.

Height/spread 25x8m (82x26ft) after 15–20 years

Life expectancy 60 years

Soil type Chalk, clay, loam, sand; acid, alkaline or neutral; moist but well-drained

Native to Europe, southwest Asia and northern Africa

Hardiness H7

HAZEL

Corylus avellana

A lovely small tree and brilliantly versatile, hazel can be grown as a multi-stemmed shrub, standard tree, as part of a hedge, or coppiced. Its fresh green leaves and multi-stemmed habit make it a perfect choice for a woodland border while, if grown as a small tree or shrub, hazel has a lovely shape. It's fast growing and will quickly fill its space.

Both male and female flowers appear on the same tree. Male flowers are long, yellow catkins, while female flowers are tiny – look for fine red styles or threads protruding from a green bud, usually at the top of a cluster of male catkins. Hazel is wind pollinated, but the male catkins also provide pollen for early bees. Hazel is a useful habitat for many other wild species, including the caterpillars of the large emerald, small white wave, barred umber and nut-tree tussock moths. A large number of birds and mammals enthusiastically consume its nuts, including the aptly named hazel dormouse.

Hazel has long been associated with coppicing – a traditional way of managing woodland. Young stems are cut close to the ground to promote growth of new shoots. These shoots are harvested after a few years, starting the cycle again. Coppicing brings light to the woodland floor, allowing spring flowers to bloom, while providing fuel and young, straight stems for walking sticks, bean poles and basket weaving.

CARE NOTES

Very little care is needed if you leave your hazel to grow naturally. If you want to coppice your tree to manage its size, or even to use its stems in the garden, simply cut back all the stems to around 5cm (2in) from the ground in February or March. Repeat every few years once strong new shoots have formed. Trim hazel hedges in late winter, before growth starts in spring. Never let the soil around hazel dry out completely – water in very dry weather if there is a long, dry spell.

Height/spread 8x8m (26x26ft) but often smaller if clipped as a hedge or coppiced

Life expectancy 80 years, longer if coppiced

Soil type Chalk, loam, sand; alkaline or neutral; moist but well-drained

Native to Europe including the British Isles

Hardiness H6

ID NOTES

Leaves Heart-shaped, ribbed and toothed, fresh green and soft with hairs on the underside; yellow in autumn

Twigs Bendy and hairy

Flowers Male catkins like lambs' tails, and bright red, string-like female flowers, on the same plant, appearing in late winter

Fruit/seed Edible nuts encased in a leafy husk

Bark Smooth, grey-brown, peels with age

Leaf

Nuts

Female flower

Male catkins

ID NOTES

Leaves Oval, pale green with slightly hairy undersides

Twigs Red-brown to green

Flowers Large fluffy yellow catkins before the leaves burst

Fruit/seed Small capsules, each containing seeds encased in white fluff

Bark Smooth, grey

Leaf

Catkins

Salix caprea 'Kilmarnock'

TREE PROFILES

KILMARNOCK WILLOW

Salix caprea **'Kilmarnock'**

There are around 400 types of willow tree in the *Salix* genus. Many are enormous and far too big to grow in the average garden; you'll find them along riverbanks where they thrive in the damp soil. But the Kilmarnock willow is a notable exception, and has many beautiful features that make it a dream for a smaller garden.

Technically a goat willow grafted onto another willow species, the Kilmarnock willow has a weeping habit. It will never grow more than 2.5m (8ft) tall and provides much of the wildlife value of larger willows, but in a small space. Grow it in a sunny spot, where it will put on the best display of catkins. Several species of moth use it, while bumblebees, solitary bees and some species of fly flock to it for the pollen- and nectar-rich catkins in early spring. It's a hugely important source of food for pollinators as it flowers earlier than many other spring-flowering plants.

Another willow suitable for smaller gardens is *S. alba* var. *vitellina* 'Britzensis'. While its parent, *S. alba*, grows to 25m (82ft) tall or more, and needs wet soil to thrive, 'Britzensis' is cultivated for garden use, tolerating clay and damp sites, but not dry ones. It is usually cut in early spring to make the most of its bright red shoots, which are more colourful when young. It's ideal for the winter garden.

CARE NOTES

Water regularly for the first couple of years. Otherwise little care is needed apart from removing dead or damaged stems (see pp.158–59). Older trees may need thinning as growth becomes congested. To do this, remove whole stems back to the main framework of branches in spring – avoid shortening stems part of the way as this will encourage lots of shoots and make congestion worse, and you could end up with a very unnatural-looking tree that appears to have had a severe haircut. To prune the variety 'Britzensis' for its bright, young shoots, cut shoots in late winter or spring to 5–8cm (2–3in) from the ground, then repeat annually or every few years, cutting to the previous stubs.

Height/spread 1.8x2.5m (6x8ft) after 20 years

Life expectancy 50 years

Soil type Clay, loam, sand; acid, alkaline or neutral; moist but well-drained

----

Native to Temperate regions of Europe and North America

Hardiness H6

SILVER BIRCH

Betula pendula

A beautiful, deciduous tree with a conical shape, silver birch grows to 20m (66ft). Unlike many trees its height isn't imposing as it has a light canopy, letting sunlight filter through its gently weeping branches, and small leaves. It has elegant, peeling white bark, which develops dark, diamond-shaped fissures with age. In autumn its leaves turn a gorgeous, buttery yellow, before falling.

Popular with wildlife, silver birch is loved by tits, which feast on seeds from its brown seed pods, and pick through its branches for caterpillars and other insects. Redpolls and finches eat its seeds, too. It tolerates pollution, making it a good choice for city gardens.

In spring, as the tree starts to come into leaf, you can press your ear against a bare section of trunk and listen to the sap rising in the tree. It's said to sound like a fast-flowing river. The sap (often called birch water) has been consumed by people for centuries straight from the tree; it is nutrient rich, and believed to have many medicinal properties. To "tap" a birch for its sap, choose one with a trunk diameter of 25cm (10in), and drill a hole in the trunk 3cm (1in) deep and about 1m (3ft) from the ground, in an upward-facing direction. Use a piece of hosepipe or similar to direct the sap into a container. Avoid tapping the tree every year – give it a couple of years' rest between tapping.

Other birches that make good garden trees include the ornamental Himalayan birch (*B. utilis*), and the Chinese red birch (*B. albosinensis*).

CARE NOTES

Very little care is needed, although formative pruning in autumn or winter may be necessary to remove lower branches if you want a single-stemmed tree (see pp.157–58). Don't allow the soil to dry out – mulching annually will help to conserve soil moisture.

Height/spread 20x8m (65x26ft) after 50 years

Life expectancy 80 years

Soil type Chalk, clay, loam, sand; acid, alkaline or neutral; moist but well-drained

----

Native to Europe and Asia, including the British Isles

Hardiness H7

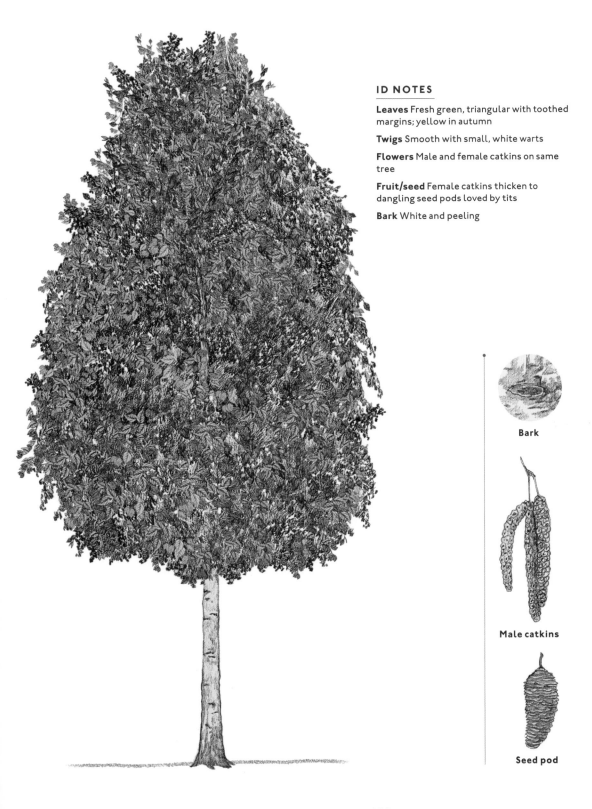

ID NOTES

Leaves Fresh green, triangular with toothed margins; yellow in autumn

Twigs Smooth with small, white warts

Flowers Male and female catkins on same tree

Fruit/seed Female catkins thicken to dangling seed pods loved by tits

Bark White and peeling

Bark

Male catkins

Seed pod

Seed- and nut-bearing trees

ID NOTES

Leaves Oblong, glossy and with parallel veins; yellow in autumn

Twigs Purple-brown with oval, plum-coloured buds

Flowers Male and female catkins are long and yellow and found on the same tree

Fruit/seed Sweet chestnuts wrapped in a prickly husk known as a burr

Bark Grey-purple and smooth, develops deep grooves with age

Chestnuts

Catkins and leaves

Twig

TREE PROFILES

SWEET CHESTNUT

Castanea sativa

Related to oaks and beeches, the sweet chestnut is a large deciduous tree, suitable only for large gardens. It's a majestic-looking tree, with smooth grey-purple bark that develops deep ridges with age. The best thing about it, though, is its chestnuts, which are traditionally roasted on "an open fire" at Christmas.

Each spiky chestnut case holds two to three chestnuts, which are smaller and lighter brown than the inedible horse chestnut, *Aesculus hippocastanum* (see pp.120–21). The flowers are visited by pollinators in spring, while squirrels eat the nuts. Several species of moth use its leaves as a foodplant.

The sweet chestnut was introduced to Britain by the Romans, who used the nuts to make a sort of porridge. In London's Greenwich Park there are 52 sweet chestnut trees thought to date back to the mid-1600s.

Harvest sweet chestnuts in October when they drop from the tree, the burrs (outer spiny skins) bursting, and the nuts spilling out as they land. Some need removing from their skin – you may want to wear thick gloves for this as the burrs are very spiny. Either freeze them or eat them as soon as you have harvested them, as they dry out quickly. They can be eaten raw (when they're crunchy) or roasted, which softens them. They are also used in stuffing mixtures, and in stews, soups and more substantial meals.

CARE NOTES

Choose a sunny spot to ensure the maximum number of nuts are produced. Bear in mind that trees may take 20 years to bear fruit – though some varieties such as 'Marron de Lyon' will bear fruit after just two or three years. Water well until it becomes established and mulch annually with well-rotted manure or compost.

Height/spread 35x10m (115x33ft) after 50 years.

Life expectancy 600 years

Soil type Loam, sand; acid or neutral; well-drained

Native to Southern Europe and parts of Asia

Hardiness H6

Seed- and nut-bearing trees

ALMOND

Prunus dulcis

Almonds make fantastic ornamental trees, with gorgeous, soft pink spring blossom. They have been cultivated for thousands of years. The tree was introduced to California in the 1800s, and the state now produces some 80 per cent of the world's almonds, although there are serious concerns as to the sustainability of almond production in California owing to the severe droughts experienced there in recent years – almonds are thirsty trees.

In the British Isles almonds are unlikely to bear fruit, as their early flowers are susceptible to spring frosts. They do best where winters are mild and summers are hot. However, there are almond trees that do well in the urban heat islands of central London, and other large cities, and which do bear fruit (and therefore almonds). Unless you choose a self-fertile variety such as 'Robijn', you'll need a male and female tree for any chance of success. But they are worth it for the blossom alone, and – you never know – you may be lucky with fruit. Grow your almond in a very sheltered, sunny spot, as you would a peach or nectarine.

The fragrant almond nuts are used in baking, confectionery and "mylk", a milk-like liquid made from blending soaked almonds. Oil from the nut is used in cosmetics.

CARE NOTES

Choose a St Julien or Montclair rootstock for a maximum height of around 4.5m (15ft). Pruning takes place in late summer and is not dissimilar to that of apple trees – after planting, cut back branches by one-third to promote a bushy shape. Over time, prune to create an open centre so that light and air can reach the developing fruits (see pp.160–61). Trees may be susceptible to leaf curl – the only way to manage this is to pick off and destroy infected leaves in spring. Keep young trees well watered in dry periods.

Height/spread 8x4m (26x13ft) after 20–50 years

Life expectancy 50 years

Soil type Chalk, clay, loam, sand; acid, alkaline or neutral; moist but well-drained

Native to Iran and surrounding countries

Hardiness H6

ID NOTES

Leaves Oblong, with prominent veining; yellow in autumn

Twigs Grey and smooth with alternate, reddish flower buds

Flowers Bright pink, star-shaped

Fruit/seed Oblong, furry-textured case, containing an almond

Bark Grey-brown and fissured

Nuts

Flower

LARGE
TREES

Suitable only for large gardens, this selection of trees consists mostly of British native deciduous trees, such as oak, beech and lime. They're absolutely worth growing if you have the space, but need some careful planning as to where they will live. The largest trees range in height from 20m (66ft) to some 45m (148ft), with the spread of the tree sometimes eventually matching its height. They take time to mature, and you'll never see your tree reach its final height and spread, but many generations will enjoy it – some large trees can live for over 1,000 years!

YEW

Taxus baccata

Often found in churchyards, yew is
a coniferous tree that can become
enormous, but also makes a fine
hedging and topiary plant.

Yews can be grown as single- or multi-
stemmed trees, providing year-round,
evergreen interest for us, flowers for
pollinators, and bright red berries for birds
and small mammals. All parts are toxic to
humans, but particularly the seeds, and
should not be eaten. Birds and mammals
can pass the seeds through their digestive
system without being harmed. Grown as
a hedge or large topiary form, yew offers
a green foil for colourful plants. Its dense
foliage helps hide unsightly views, and
provides nesting for birds. Yew is one
of Europe's longest-lived plants.

Fruit

Flower

Height/spread 15m (49ft) after
20–50 years

Life expectancy 3,000 years

Soil type Loam, chalk, clay, sand; acid or
neutral; well-drained

Native to Europe and North Africa

Hardiness H7

ID NOTES

Leaves Dark green, pointed needles

Twigs Dark green

Flowers Male and female flowers grow on
different trees, in spring; male flowers
off-white, small and round; female flowers
look like green, scaly buds

Fruit/seed Small red drupe containing one
hard seed

Bark Reddish-brown, fissured and peeling

CARE NOTES

Water well as yew establishes, then you
won't need to water it again. Yew needs very
little care and no pruning. However, topiary
and hedges need regular trimming to form
and maintain size and shape (see pp.158–60).

ID NOTES

Leaves Fresh green, oval in shape and ribbed; yellow/orange in autumn

Twigs Slender and grey with alternate, torpedo-shaped buds

Flowers Insignificant, rounded catkins; the male catkin is slightly smaller and darker

Fruit/seed Beech "mast" forms as small, hard-shelled fruit with a spiky surface and angled, glossy brown seeds inside

Bark Smooth and grey

Autumn leaf

Mast

Flower

Twig

BEECH

Fagus sylvatica

Common beech is one of the most beautiful woodland trees. Its fresh, green, slightly hairy leaves mark spring, before ageing to a darker green and losing their furry coat. They develop an orangey hue with age and then turn a glorious russet before falling in autumn. The smooth, grey bark is the perfect foil for all this leafy beauty.

Beech trees are excellent for wildlife: their leaves are eaten by the caterpillars of several species of moth, the mast (seeds) are eaten by mice, voles, squirrels and birds. As they age they provide homes for nesting birds and squirrels, and the bark is often home to fungi, mosses and lichens. Mature trees shed masses of leaves in autumn, that are perfect for making leaf mould. The mast root readily into pots and garden borders.

If you love beech trees but don't have space for a tree, then a beech hedge could be a good option for you. Young beech trees hold onto their leaves in winter, and the pruning process keeps hedges in their juvenile state so they retain their leaves all year round, forming a really effective screen even in winter. Beech hedges are things of beauty – formal yet soft, with the winter leaves ensuring they look good all year.

CARE NOTES

Keep well watered for the first couple of years after planting. Beech trees need very little care but hedges need regular pruning (see pp.158–60). Formative pruning should be done in winter but, once established, prune in late summer (after birds have finished nesting). Taper hedges slightly so the base is wider than the top – this ensures light reaches all parts of the hedge.

Height/spread 40x20m (131x66ft) after 20–50 years

Life expectancy 600 years

Soil type Chalk, clay, loam, sand; acid, alkaline, neutral; moist but well-drained

----

Native to Europe and the southeast of the British Isles

Hardiness H6

ENGLISH OAK

Quercus robur

Our common oak, known as English oak, is one of two native British species of oak (and the more dominant of the two). A further three species have been naturalised in the British Isles and there are about 600 around the world. Related to the beech, the English oak is a large, majestic tree, with characteristic lobed leaves and acorn fruits.

The English oak supports more life than any other British tree species, including hundreds of types of insect, which in turn are food for birds and their young, plus mammals and other insects. Birds such as jays feast on its acorns, while holes and crevices in the bark are used by other birds, bats and squirrels. The English oak is host to fungi such as fly agaric, cep and chicken of the woods. Its rotting leaves offer opportunities for detritivores such as centipedes, ground beetles, caterpillars, and even mammals.

Oaks can on occasion live for up to 1,000 years. As they age, their crown starts to die back, allowing light to reach the inner crown, which stimulates growth and eventually results in a new, smaller crown developing. The old branches die off but can remain on the tree, giving the tree a "stag-headed" appearance.

Fantastic garden trees, oaks are suitable only for very large gardens. Plant an oak and think of those who will enjoy it in 200, 500 and even 1,000 years' time.

CARE NOTES

An oak tree needs little care after planting, but water it regularly in its first two years. You can expect your English oak to grow to around 10m (33ft) tall after 20 years, and it will only start producing acorns after this time.

Height/spread 35x10m (115x33ft) after 50 years

Life expectancy 1,000 years

Soil type Chalk, clay loam, sand; acid, alkaline or neutral; moist but well-drained

Native to Temperate regions of Europe and North America

Hardiness H6

TREE PROFILES

ID NOTES

Leaves Round-lobed leaves with short stalks; yellow in autumn

Twigs Green-brown, with clusters of buds at the tip

Flowers Long yellow catkins

Fruit/seed Green acorns (fruits sitting in a "cup"), which age to brown

Bark Medium brown, developing fissures with age

Autumn leaf

Bark

Flowers

Acorn

ID NOTES

Leaves Palmate, with five to seven oval, ribbed leaflets; red/brown in autumn

Twigs Red-brown with sticky, rounded buds

Flowers Candle-like spires of individual white florets, tinged pink

Seeds Hard conker encased in a spiky green shell

Bark Smooth, pink-grey when young, developing fissures with age

Autumn leaf

Twig

Conker

TREE PROFILES

HORSE CHESTNUT

Aesculus hippocastanum

The horse chestnut, or conker tree, is a stalwart of children's story books and playground history. Its conkers have been used in conker fights for generations, with children seeking out the biggest, shiniest conkers, forcing holes into them and then looping string through them so they could bash each other with them in school breaks – now a practice discouraged in schools.

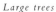

Conker trees are a thing of beauty. Tall and majestic, their fresh green leaves and candelabra-like flowers mark the coming of spring, while their conkers tell us that autumn has arrived. When the leaves fall in autumn, they leave a scar on the twig they detached from, which resembles an inverted horseshoe complete with nail holes, giving the tree its common name.

While it is native to the Balkans, the horse chestnut is considered naturalised to the British Isles. Its flowers are visited by a number of pollinators, and a couple of moths use its leaves as a caterpillar foodplant. Large mammals eat the conkers.

In recent years, the horse chestnut has been affected by the horse chestnut leaf mining moth, a southern European species first found in Britain in 2002. It lays its eggs on the leaves and its larvae mine inside, eating them from within. Brown or white blotches are visible on the leaves. Heavily affected trees can drop leaves early, but this appears not to affect its vigour. Blue tits eat the larvae and their cocoons, so could provide some long-term natural control for the moth.

CARE NOTES

Very little care is needed beyond formative pruning, where crossing, dead and low-growing branches should be removed (see pp.158–59). Water for the first two years when conditions are dry.

Height/spread 40x20m (131x66ft) after 20–50 years

Life expectancy 300 years

Soil type Loam, sand; acid, neutral; moist but well-drained

Native to The Balkans

Hardiness H7

SMALL-LEAVED LIME

Tilia cordata

The small-leaved lime is a huge deciduous tree, suitable only for large gardens. That said, it's a wonderful specimen if you do have a large garden. Its fresh-green leaves make the perfect spring spectacle, its fragrant flowers attract bees, and its leaves are used by a range of moths, including the gorgeous lime hawk moth.

Because small-leaved lime trees are so long-lived, they provide dead wood for wood-boring beetles, and nesting holes for birds. Aphids are attracted to lime trees, providing a source of food for birds, and insect predators such as hoverflies and ladybirds. Bees even drink aphid honeydew from the leaves in spring. Beware: honeydew from aphids can be an issue, and anything beneath your lime tree – such as a car or garden furniture – could have a dressing of honeydew before long!

Lime trees have a gruesome, slightly macabre relationship with bees, in that the nectar of some species, particularly the silver lime (*Tilia tomentosa*), is thought to kill them. For years, dead bees (usually bumblebees) have been observed beneath lime trees. It's thought the nectar in the flowers is toxic to bees. It's not fully understood how or why this happens. Some have suggested that, in a dry spring, certain compounds are more concentrated in the nectar, making it more toxic. Small-leaved lime isn't considered to be one of the dangerous limes to bees, so consider it a bee-friendly tree for a large garden. But do keep it well watered, just in case!

CARE NOTES

Water in dry periods. Formative prune young trees by removing crossing, dead and low-growing branches (see pp.158–59). It will take 20-50 years to reach its maximum height, depending on growing conditions.

Height/spread 25x20m (82x66ft) after 50 years

Life expectancy 200 years

Soil type Chalk, clay, sand; alkaline or neutral; moist but well-drained

Native to Europe

Hardiness H6

ID NOTES

Leaves Heart-shaped, bright green with a pointed tip; yellow in autumn

Twigs Reddish on top and olive green below

Flowers Green/yellow "fluffy" hermaphrodite (male and female parts are contained within the same flower)

Fruit/seed Rounded with oval tips

Bark Grey-brown and smooth, developing flaky plates with age

Leaf

Twig

Flower

Seed

TREES FOR
AUTUMN COLOUR

The leaves of many deciduous trees change colour before
falling in autumn (see pp.42–43), but some look truly
spectacular. So, if you're looking for a tree that wows in
autumn, look no further. Inevitably, as in other categories
in this book, this list of trees isn't exhaustive, and you'll find
trees in other parts of the book with excellent autumn colour
(cherry trees, in the Fruit tree section, and beech, in the
Large trees section, both look glorious as their leaves turn).
However, this section is made up of trees that are particularly
known for their autumn leaf colouring, such as the
wonderful sweet gum and Japanese maple.

TREE PROFILES

Cercis canadensis
'Forest Pansy'

Height/spread 5x5m (16x16ft) after 20 years

Life expectancy 70 years

Soil type Loam, sand; acid or neutral; moist but well-drained

Native to North America

Hardiness H5

Twig

Flower

REDBUD

Cercis canadensis

A gorgeous tree for a small garden, redbud is native to eastern North America, including Canada. The species has beautiful heart-shaped leaves and pink, pea-like flowers.

Arguably the best garden variety is 'Forest Pansy'. Its flowers appear in spring on bare wood, followed by bright red, heart-shaped leaves that darken to a lustrous purple. In autumn the leaves colour further, turning vibrant shades of orange, red, yellow and purple. It looks spectacular and ethereal when backlit by the sun, so choose your planting position wisely to make the most of this effect. For wildlife, the redbud doesn't disappoint – its flowers are loved by bees, particularly in its native area, and leafcutter bees use its leaves to line their nests.

ID NOTES

Leaves Heart-shaped, bright red; in autumn deep, dark red, orange, yellow and purple

Twigs Dark brown and speckled

Flowers Pink, pea-like, borne in clusters

Seeds Pea-like pods with flattened, brown seeds

Bark Red-brown with deep fissures

CARE NOTES

Very little pruning is necessary, apart from the removal of crossing or dead branches (see pp.158–59). Keep the soil moist, but not boggy, while the tree is establishing. Mulch annually in autumn to help retain moisture.

ID NOTES

Leaves Palmate with five-, seven- or nine-pointed lobes; orange-red, purple and gold in autumn

Twigs Variable, but always bearing opposite buds

Flowers Borne in small, red hanging clusters

Seeds Paired samara (winged seeds)

Bark Varied

Leaf

Flower

Seed

Acer japonicum

TREE PROFILES

JAPANESE MAPLE

Acer **spp.**

Available in a huge variety of shapes and sizes, Japanese maples are prized for their fantastic autumn colour, compact, graceful size and slow-growing habit, making them an excellent choice for small gardens. They also grow well in pots. They require very little pruning and, as long as they're in a sheltered spot away from drying winter winds, they will last for years, providing many seasons of colour and interest.

There's a range of Japanese maples to choose from – all have spectacular autumn colour. Some, such as *Acer palmatum* var. *dissectum* also have delicate, filigree leaves, while others such as coral bark maples (*A. p.* 'Sango-kaku') have interesting bark that is a focal point in winter.

Choose your Japanese maple carefully – *A. japonicum* grows as a small tree, while *A. palmatum* is more shrub-like, as it grows broader than it does tall. All species are slow growing, so buy the largest specimen you can afford. Most Japanese maples grow best in shade or partial shade, especially variegated types, which may suffer leaf scorch if they receive too much sun. For sunnier situations, opt for a green-leaved maple that develops red or purple autumn leaf colour, as it needs some sun for the colourful pigments to develop fully.

Because they're compact and slow growing, Japanese maples work well in pots. Grow in a good soil-based compost such as John Innes No. 3 or a peat-free ericaceous compost with added sharp sand to aid drainage, and keep the compost moist but not saturated.

CARE NOTES

Japanese maples need very little care, but you may need to prune to remove crossing or dead branches from time to time (see pp.158–59). Always prune when dormant (in winter) to prevent "bleeding" (losing sap). Mulch annually in spring to retain soil moisture.

Height/spread 10x8m (33x26ft) after 10–20 years

Life expectancy 100 years

Soil type Loam; acid, slightly alkaline or neutral; well-drained

Native to East Asia

Hardiness H7–H2; H6 for *A. japonicum* and *A. palmatum*

MAIDENHAIR TREE

Ginkgo biloba

A window into an old world, the maidenhair or ginkgo tree dates back 270 million years. Neither a conifer nor a broadleaf tree, it sits on its own in the Ginkgophyta division of the plant kingdom – all of its relatives in this division are extinct. *Ginkgo biloba* can live for up to 3,000 years. It is the National Tree of China, and it's said that there are ginkgos planted in temples there that are more than 2,500 years old.

Slow-growing and relatively compact, the maidenhair tree is perfect for a small garden. It's hardy and conical, but gently spreads with age. The main attraction is the leaves, which are unusual, fan-shaped and with no visible leaf veins. They often split in the centre, forming two lobes, earning its name *biloba*. Its common name refers to the leaves' resemblance to those of the maidenhair fern. They turn a glorious shade of yellow in autumn.

Trees are either male or female (dioecious). Female flowers are followed by ball-shaped fruits, said to smell of rancid butter. It's almost impossible to tell male and female gingko trees apart until the female tree is in flower, so if you're determined to avoid a female, it's best not to grow a gingko at all. It grows in most conditions and makes a fine street tree as it's extremely pollution tolerant. Grow it in a sunny spot as a focal point of the garden or as part of an ornamental border.

Ginkgos are prized for their medicinal properties. The leaves contain ginkgolides, which are used in medicines to improve blood circulation to the brain and are said to relieve symptoms of Alzheimer's, tinnitus and Raynaud syndrome.

CARE NOTES

Ginkgo is incredibly easy to care for. It requires no pruning and is susceptible to no pests or diseases. However, it needs full sun to thrive and will suffer in shade. Mulch annually in autumn or spring to retain soil moisture.

Height/spread 10x4m (33x13ft) after 20 years

Life expectancy 3,000 years

Soil type Chalk, clay, loam, sand; acid, alkaline or neutral; moist but well-drained

Native to China

Hardiness H6

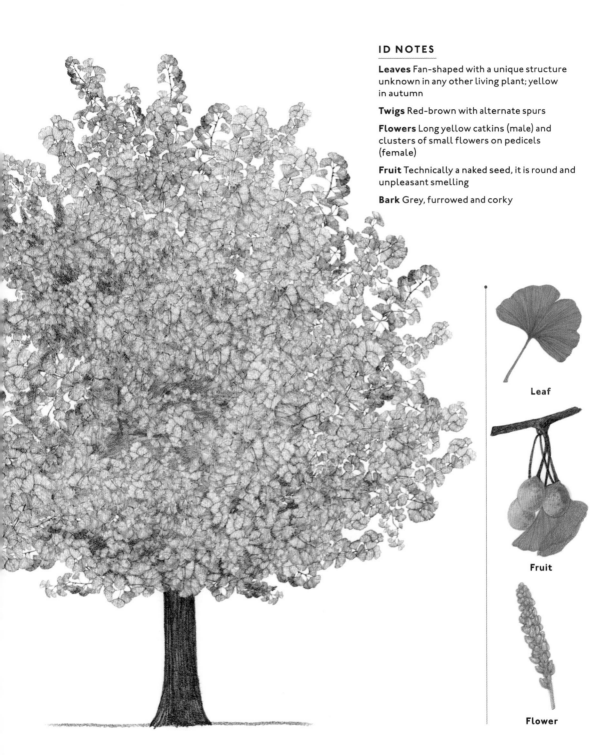

ID NOTES

Leaves Fan-shaped with a unique structure unknown in any other living plant; yellow in autumn

Twigs Red-brown with alternate spurs

Flowers Long yellow catkins (male) and clusters of small flowers on pedicels (female)

Fruit Technically a naked seed, it is round and unpleasant smelling

Bark Grey, furrowed and corky

Leaf

Fruit

Flower

SWEET GUM

Liquidambar styraciflua

One of the most beautiful trees you can plant in your garden, sweet gum has magnificent autumn colour, with leaves turning shades of red, purple, yellow and orange, before falling. Grey, ridged bark adds winter interest. Plant your sweet gum in the sunniest part of your garden for the most dramatic autumn colour, and make sure it's in the perfect spot to see it in its full glory.

With a reasonable growth rate and a conical habit when young (more rounded with age), sweet gum is perfect for smaller gardens, where it makes a striking focal point. Birds and squirrels eat the fruits and may use mature trees for nesting. Being wind-pollinated, the male flowers are packed with pollen and attract bees. The only downside is the hard, spiky seed pods, which can cause injury if you slip or fall on them, and are hard to rake up.

Sweet gum takes its name from the sweet, sticky resin that is sometimes exuded from the bark. Historically, this was used in folk medicine and has also been used to make chewing gum. There are several cultivars available, including 'Worplesdon', which has a conical shape, 'Andrew Hewson', which is smaller than the species, and 'Happydaze', which is sterile and so doesn't produce the spiky seed pods. Other cultivars have features such as variegated leaves.

CARE NOTES

Sweet gum is largely free of pests and diseases. Pruning isn't necessary, but do remove damaged, crossing or diseased stems (see pp.158–59). Water well as it becomes established, particularly in prolonged dry spells. Mulch annually, in spring or autumn, to retain soil moisture.

Height/spread 10x6m (33x20ft) after 20 years

Life expectancy 150 years

Soil type Clay, loam, sand; acid to slightly alkaline; moist but well-drained

Native to Southeastern USA and the cloud forests of Central America

Hardiness H6

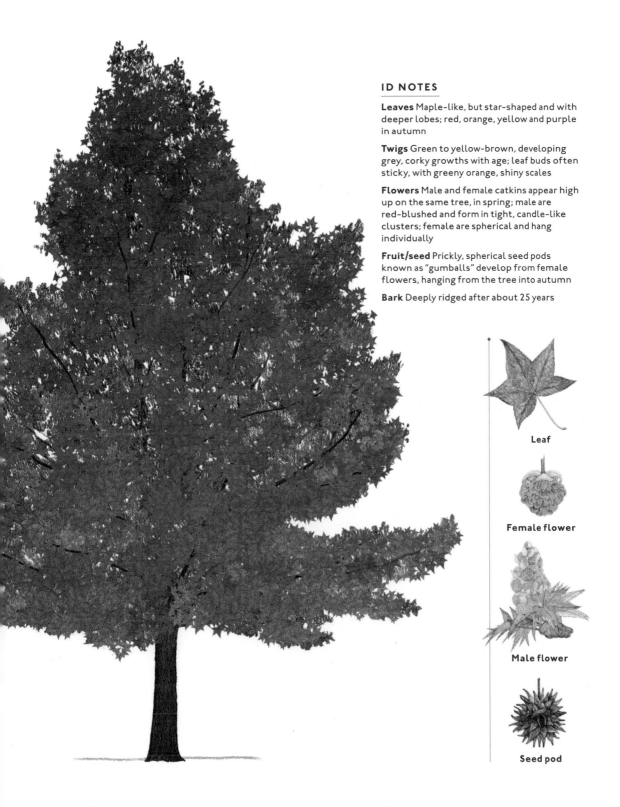

ID NOTES

Leaves Maple-like, but star-shaped and with deeper lobes; red, orange, yellow and purple in autumn

Twigs Green to yellow-brown, developing grey, corky growths with age; leaf buds often sticky, with greeny orange, shiny scales

Flowers Male and female catkins appear high up on the same tree, in spring; male are red-blushed and form in tight, candle-like clusters; female are spherical and hang individually

Fruit/seed Prickly, spherical seed pods known as "gumballs" develop from female flowers, hanging from the tree into autumn

Bark Deeply ridged after about 25 years

Leaf

Female flower

Male flower

Seed pod

ID NOTES

Leaves Large, oval, green glossy; red, orange and yellow in autumn

Twigs Red-brown to grey, with pointed buds, darkening to brown in the winter

Flowers Borne in tiny, green-white clusters

Fruit Blue-purple berries

Bark Dark grey and flaky, developing furrows with age

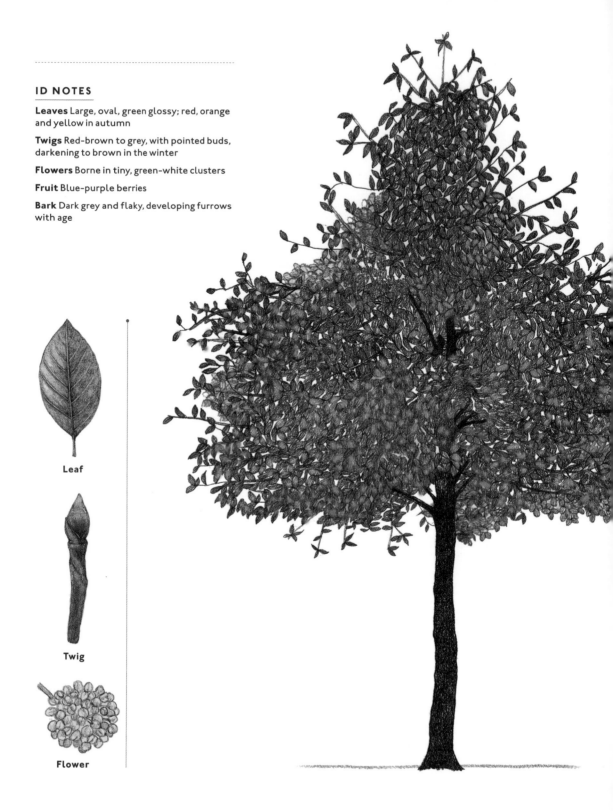

Leaf

Twig

Flower

TREE PROFILES

BLACK TUPELO

Nyssa sylvatica

This beautiful small tree has glossy, green leaves that turn incredible shades of orange, red and yellow in autumn, rivalling Japanese maple but growing to a more impressive size – though it still works well in a small garden. Its deep purple berries look beautiful against the backdrop of autumn leaves, and birds eat them, too.

Black tupelo has a pleasing conical shape, growing symmetrically to just 5x4m (16x13ft) over 20 years or so. It does best in full sun to partial shade. It thrives in a moist, acidic soil and will do particularly well in heavy clay soils. On drier soils it will need lots of additional watering, so you're better off choosing a Japanese maple (see pp.126–27). There are several cultivars available, including 'Jermyns Flame', which has particularly striking autumn colour.

For a lesser-known, but possibly even more dramatic-looking tree, choose the Chinese tupelo (*Nyssa sinensis*). Smaller than its American cousin, it's ideal for urban gardens and makes a fine street tree, too. Grown as a tree or large shrub, it bears bronze foliage that develops fiery red, orange and yellow colouring before falling in autumn. Its flowers are inconspicuous clusters of green and white, and its berries are fairly unremarkable, too. This tree is grown purely for its foliage, which is as dramatic as it comes. Like the black tupelo, the Chinese tupelo is also better suited to moist soils, and can be grown near a pond or stream.

CARE NOTES

Grow in a sheltered spot, away from strong winds. Tupelo trees have a long taproot, which can be damaged when it is transplanted, so it's best to plant them from young, pot-grown plants only. Avoid pruning unless absolutely necessary, and keep well watered in the first couple of years.

Height/spread 8x8m (26x26ft) after 50 years

Life expectancy 70 years

Soil type Loam, sand; acid or neutral; moist but well-drained (tolerates boggy soil for short periods)

Native to North America

Hardiness H6

STAG'S HORN SUMACH

Rhus typhina

A small tree or shrub, this is dramatic in ornamental borders and container displays alike. It has large green pinnate leaves that turn glorious shades of red and orange in autumn.

Female trees bear beautiful clusters of berries that persist into winter. The berries are eaten by a number of bird species in its native North America. They're edible for us, too. Although *Rhus typhina* isn't one of the *Rhus* species used for making the sumac spice (typically used in Mediterranean cuisine and one of the main ingredients in za'atar), the dried berries can be ground to make a passable substitute. This tree grows well in a container, which also helps deal with its tendency to sucker (see below).

ID NOTES

Leaves Large, pinnate; red and orange in autumn

Twigs Stout, reddish-brown and fuzzy

Flowers Cone-shaped yellow clusters

Fruit/seed Cone-shaped clusters of red berries

Bark Grey-brown and scaly

Flower

Fruit

CARE NOTES

In the British Isles sumach has a tendency to sucker (send out new shoots from the roots), which can be a problem in small gardens. A pot will contain its suckering tendencies, and also produce a smaller tree. You can "containerise" the tree in the ground by placing an impermeable membrane – such as paving slabs – around the roots. Cut off any suckers that appear. Avoid growing it near lawns or boundaries.

Height/spread Up to 8x8m (26x26ft) after 20 years

Life expectancy 50 years

Soil type Loam, sand; acid, alkaline or neutral; moist but well-drained

Native to North America

Hardiness H6

PAPERBARK MAPLE

Acer griseum

One of the most glorious trees you can grow in a small garden, the paperbark maple comes into its own over the autumn months, when its leaves turn fiery shades of red and orange.

The beautiful papery, peeling bark (which earns the paperbark its name) steals the show throughout winter. Choose a spot for planting, where you can see it from indoors and appreciate its beauty even when it's too cold to venture outside.

Paperbark maple is a slow-growing tree, and will take 20 years or more to reach its full size. Its nectar-rich flowers are attractive to pollinators, which include birds in its native China.

Height/spread 12x8m (39x26ft) after 20 years

Life expectancy 150 years

Soil type Loam, sand; acid, alkaline or neutral; moist but well-drained

Native to China

Hardiness H5

Leaf

Seed

Flower

ID NOTES

Leaves Palmate with three green leaflets; orange-red in autumn

Twigs Slender and brown with light spots (lenticels) and dark brown, sharply pointed buds

Flowers Clusters of small, green hanging flowers

Seeds Paired samara (winged seeds)

Bark Peeling, like paper

CARE NOTES

Grow in a sheltered spot. There should be no reason to prune, but remove dead or crossing branches (see pp.158–59) on both young and older trees when the tree is dormant (winter) as it can bleed sap if pruned at other times of year. Mulch in spring to retain soil moisture.

PALM
TREES

Palms are often overlooked as garden trees. While they
usually don't absorb as much carbon dioxide as other types
of tree (owing to the comparative lack of leaf cover), and are
much less attractive to native wildlife, they do still have a
role in gardens – whether that's as an evergreen focal point
or part of a tropical plant display. Palm trees come in a range
of shapes and sizes and many are compact, making them
a reliable choice for a small plot. Many are also salt- and
wind-tolerant, so are a good option if you live near the coast.
Most palms need tropical or subtropical temperatures to
thrive, but some can be grown outdoors in the British Isles;
bear in mind that most will grow smaller in our gardens than
in their native, tropical regions. Hardy palms make excellent
structural plants in tropical displays and work well when
planted with bananas, bamboos and New Zealand flax.

CABBAGE PALM

Cordyline australis

The cabbage palm is not a true palm; it's tall and often single trunked, although branching can sometimes occur after flowering.

In summer the cabbage palm bears masses of fragrant white flowers, beloved by bees, and its berries are eaten by birds, particularly starlings. It has large evergreen rosettes of long, sword-shaped dark green leaves. One of the easiest exotic trees to grow, it's a good choice for a coastal location and is hardy down to -9°C (16°F). For small gardens, it will grow happily in a pot, although bear in mind that its height will be restricted in a container – it may reach only 2m (6½ft) tall – and you'll need to repot it from time to time, which can be tricky for large specimens.

ID NOTES

Leaves Sword-shaped, green, borne in clusters

Flowers Cream-white, fragrant panicles

Fruit Clusters of white berries

Bark Corky and grey

Height/spread 8x4m (26x13ft) after 20–50 years

Life expectancy 50–100 years

Soil type Loam, sand, chalk, clay; acid, alkaline or neutral; moist but well-drained

Native to New Zealand

Hardiness H3

Bark

Fruit

CARE NOTES

Cabbage palms need little regular pruning, but respond well to renovation pruning, whereby you cut the tree right back to the ground in spring to encourage new growth or change its shape. You can also tidy it from time to time, removing old, dead or straggly leaves. Pot-grown cabbage palms need extra watering and the top few centimetres of the compost replacing annually. Those in large pots may never need repotting, but those in smaller containers quickly outgrow them.

CANARY ISLAND DATE PALM

Phoenix canariensis

A large palm tree, the Canary Island date palm has huge, fan-shaped green leaves and clusters of cream-yellow flowers held on long, arching stems.

Despite being native to the Canary Islands, this palm is hardy down to -6°C (21°F) and grows without problems in a sunny, sheltered spot. In its home range it can reach 15m (49ft) or more, but in cooler climates a height of 3–4m (10–13ft) is more realistic. As with many palms, its trunk develops as its old leaves fall off. Canary Island date palms come in a variety of sizes, from 1m (3ft) tall (in 20cm/8in pots) to 3m (10ft), sold in large buckets. It grows slowly, so buy the biggest one you can afford. It will grow well in a large pot.

ID NOTES

Leaves Large, fan-shaped

Flowers Small, off-white, on stalks up to 2m (6½ft) long

Fruit Yellow-orange, on female trees

Bark Fibrous

CARE NOTES

Despite being palm trees, these plants need watering in dry weather – don't let the soil around the palm dry out. If growing in pots, repot every couple of years into a slightly larger pot. When not repotting, top-dress with fresh compost, in spring. If you need to protect your palm in cold weather, use strong twine to tie all the leaves together to protect the crown.

Bark

Fruit

Height/spread 12x8m (39x26ft) after 20–50 years

Life expectancy 50–150 years

Soil type Loam; acid or neutral; well-drained

Native to Canary Islands

Hardiness H2

MEDITERRANEAN FAN PALM

Chamaerops humilis

This palm is easy to grow as long as it's planted in a sheltered, sunny spot, although it will tolerate a little shade.

The Mediterranean fan palm is native to southwestern Europe, where it reaches heights of 5m (16ft), with its leaves attaining lengths of 1.5m (5ft). However, it won't grow that big in British gardens, especially in a container, as it's incredibly slow growing. New leaves quickly develop to replace old or damaged leaves. It's hardy down to -12°C (10°F) and is tolerant of salt and wind, making it ideal for coastal gardens.

It's unlikely to bear fruit in Britain. In Spain, however, the fruit is eaten by badgers, which spread the seeds.

ID NOTES

Leaves Large, fan-shaped

Flowers Yellow, in short panicles

Fruit/seed Orange-yellow in clusters

Bark Fibrous

CARE NOTES

Water well in the first year after planting, and then afterwards water only when the rootball starts to dry out. There's usually no need to water in winter. Pruning is not needed, but you may want to remove lower leaves as they turn brown.

Bark

Fruit

Height/spread 2.5x1.5m (8x5ft) after 20–50 years

Life expectancy 50–150 years

Soil type Loam; acid or neutral; well-drained

Native to Mediterranean

Hardiness H4

CHUSAN PALM

Trachycarpus fortunei

A tall-growing palm tree, the chusan palm has a thick, fibrous trunk and fan-shaped, dark green leaves. It's perfect for growing in exotic and tropical planting schemes, and is hardy enough to survive all year round in British gardens, without protection.

Grow the chusan palm in a sunny or shady spot, in the ground or in a pot, but make sure it's sheltered – the leaves can take quite a battering from the wind. As the fibrous trunk grows, it sheds its leaves. The trunk can grow up to 30cm (12in) per year.

These palms are dioecious, meaning they bear either male or female flowers. Male flowers are tiny and yellow but appear in huge clusters, while female flowers are pale yellow and look less dramatic, and these turn into blue-black berries if there's a male tree nearby.

For a neater appearance, you can "strip" the trunk by removing the old, hairy leaves. This does not harm the plant, or make it less hardy, but reveals a smooth, pale trunk with a thinner diameter. You'll need an old bread knife or similar. Start at the bottom and use the knife to help you remove individual leaf pieces. It's a time-consuming job but many think it's worth the finished look.

CARE NOTES

Avoid planting too deeply – ensure that the base of the trunk is visible and remove any soil that piles up around it. Water well until the plant is established. Protect it from wind as this can damage the leaves and make them look unsightly.

Height/spread 12x3m (39x10ft) after 20–50 years

Life expectancy 50–150 years

Soil type Chalk, loam, sand; acid, alkaline or neutral; well-drained

Native to Southeast to Central Asia

Hardiness H5

ID NOTES

Leaves Fan-shaped, dark green up to 1m (3ft)

Flowers Yellow, borne in arching sprays

Fruit Clusters of blue-black berries

Bark Fibrous

Bark

Fruit

PINDO PALM

Butia capitata

The pindo palm is slow growing and has blue-green, fan-shaped, feathery leaves that arch from its fibrous trunk.

One of the hardiest feather palms available, it will tolerate temperatures down to -10°C (14°F). Grow it in a sheltered, sunny spot in well-drained soil. Its other common name, jelly palm, comes from the fact that its fruit is used to make jellies. However it's unlikely that the fruits will ripen in the current British climate.

Pindo palm is one of the best palms for growing in pots as its roots respond well to being restricted, and it's very slow growing. Choose a pot slightly larger than the rootball and plant into a loam-based compost such as John Innes No. 3.

Height/spread 3x3m (10x10ft) after 20–50 years

Life expectancy 80 years

Soil type Loam; acid or neutral; well-drained

Native to South America

Hardiness H4

Bark

Fruit

ID NOTES

Leaves Fan-shaped and feathery

Flowers Yellow-white, held on long, arching stems

Fruit/seed Yellow-orange fruit

Bark Fibrous

CARE NOTES

Water well until the plant is established and then only to keep the soil moist. Remove old leaves to keep it looking its best. Feed pot-grown plants with a general-purpose fertiliser every couple of weeks in the growing season. Tie the fronds over the crown to protect the tree in winter, or move potted plants indoors.

YUCCA

Yucca rostrata

A hardy palm, *Yucca rostrata* can be grown outdoors, as long as it doesn't sit in wet soil.

It's slow growing and dramatic looking, bearing masses of blue-green, sword-shaped leaves, from which an enormous flower spike appears in summer. Grow in well-drained, alkaline soil, in a sheltered, sunny spot. Make sure it can drain freely in winter – add stones to the hole when planting to increase drainage if you need to. You could also grow it in a raised bed or a pot with plenty of drainage. Pot-grown specimens can be brought outside in summer as part of an exotic container display, and then taken indoors again in autumn if you live in a particularly cold region. *Y. filamentosa* is also hardy in the UK and grows as a medium-sized shrub.

These yuccas are not to be confused with *Y. gloriosa*, which is often grown as a houseplant in the British Isles. *Y. gloriosa* has a hardiness rating of H2, so is unlikely to survive outdoors even in the mildest of British winters.

Height/spread 4x2.5m (13x8ft) after 20–50 years

Life expectancy 50–100 years

Soil type Chalk, loam, sand; alkaline or neutral / well-drained

Native to Central America

Hardiness H5

Bark

Fruit

ID NOTES

Leaves Blue-green, sword-shaped

Flowers Cream-white on a long stalk

Fruit Oblong, dark blue-brown

Bark Fibrous, comprising old, dead leaves

CARE NOTES

Water sparingly throughout summer and reduce this in autumn, stopping completely by October.

PLANT, PRUNE, CARE

Understanding the basics of planting and caring for your tree is the key to having it grow successfully. Learn how to plant bare-root and potted trees, plus essential pruning techniques and how to spot the early signs of pests and diseases, to ensure your tree will thrive for decades to come.

Choosing and planting your tree

Once you have chosen which type of tree you want to plant, you need to find a good specimen. Trees are sold in different ways and your choice may depend on your budget and the time of year you want to plant, as well as finding a good, healthy tree. You'll find a selection of trees at garden centres, but there's often a much greater range at tree nurseries and online.

When shopping for your tree, you will come across "bare-root" and "container-grown" (or "pot-grown") trees. These refer to how the trees are sold, and determine how and when you plant them. For additional considerations when buying fruit trees, see pp.150–51.

A bare-root tree
Starting life in open ground, a bare-root tree is dug up when it is dormant in autumn and winter and is sold without any soil around it – simply with its "bare roots" exposed. As it's dormant, digging it up doesn't harm it. Look for a good mass of roots that are not broken or growing in a circular shape. It's best to plant your tree straight away but if you can't then you can "heel it in" by submerging the roots in soil or sawdust for a few days to stop them drying out. Plant your tree between November and March, before it starts growing in spring. A bare-root tree is usually cheaper than a container-grown tree, and also you tend to have more varieties to choose from.

A container-grown tree
Grown and sold in a pot, as its name suggests, a container-grown tree has the advantage that it is available to buy all year round and can be planted all year too (although it's best to avoid summer when conditions are usually dry). It tends to be more expensive than a bare-root tree and you may have fewer options to choose from. But it can establish more quickly than a bare-root tree. Make sure the tree looks healthy and is not pot-bound (with roots filling the pot).

What age tree to buy

You can buy a tree at any age, but most are between one and five years old. Young trees are cheapest and establish more quickly than older trees, which can "sulk" for a couple of years after planting and not grow much. Unless you want a challenge, avoid really young trees, known as saplings, which need formative pruning and aren't robust enough to resist attack from pests such as deer and squirrels. A tree between two and four years is ideal. Young trees are mostly sold as standard trees, which have a clear stem and distinct head of branches. For guidelines about fruit trees, see pp.150–51.

When to plant a tree

Trees should be planted in soil that's moist but well drained. Frozen, dry or waterlogged soil should be avoided. Autumn is typically the best season to plant a tree as the soil is still warm from summer, and autumn rains keep the soil moist. This should lead to quick establishment of the tree, which should be able to put on root growth before entering winter dormancy, helping it to grow better come spring.

Early spring is the next best time to plant a tree, as the soil is starting to warm up and is moist after winter. There's plenty of time for the tree to establish before summer dries the soil, although it's a good idea to continue watering your tree in the first two years, especially during dry periods (see pp.152–53).

Many trees are successfully planted in winter but avoid planting your tree if the soil is frozen. You can plant a tree in summer but bear in mind that summer soils tend to be dry so you will need to water your tree regularly to ensure it establishes well.

Preparing the ground

Before planting your tree, prepare the soil thoroughly. This includes soil over a much larger area than just the planting hole to encourage the roots to spread out well. Dig over the soil and remove any weeds. Avoid adding organic matter as this will continue to break down after planting and could cause the planting area to "sink", resulting in the tree roots sitting lower in the soil than they should. Add organic matter as a mulch around the planted tree instead (see p.149). If you have very heavy clay or sandy soil then choose trees that will thrive in these conditions. Clay soil may be easier to manage if a fork is used to break up large clumps.

How to plant a tree

Your planting technique differs only slightly with bare-root and container-grown trees. Soil depth, size and shape of planting hole, and watering requirements are the same regardless of how and when you plant.

1 Soak the roots before planting. For a bare-root tree (see image), remove the wrapping and stand the roots in water for at least 30 minutes before planting. Soak pot-grown trees so the rootball is saturated.

2 Prepare the hole by digging a square hole that's wider, but not deeper, than your tree's rootball. Square holes help the roots to spread via the corners. Lightly fork the base and sides of the hole.

3 Remove the tree from its container for a pot-grown tree (see image). Gently tease out any roots of pot-grown trees that are circling around the inside of the pot. Cut off damaged roots of pot-grown or bare-root trees.

4 Position the tree by standing it in the planting hole, ensuring the top of the rootball, or "soil tide mark" on the stem of bare-root trees, sits level with the soil's surface – lay a cane over the planting hole to help you.

5 Backfill around the rootball with soil, shaking the tree gently to help the soil settle around the roots and watering well as you fill. Firm the soil gently with your heel so that there's good contact between the roots and the soil.

6 If you are staking your tree, choose a sturdy stake. Hammer it into the soil at a 45° angle, taking care to avoid any tree roots. Attach the stake to the tree trunk at one-third of the tree's height using an adjustable tree tie.

PLANT, PRUNE, CARE

Do you need to stake a tree?

Nearly all newly planted trees need staking. This prevents wind rock, which can damage the roots, reducing the amount of nutrients and water they can absorb, and making the tree vulnerable to toppling over.

There are various methods of tree staking. For most trees, a single stake attached to the tree at one-third of its height is sufficient. Ensure the stake is 60cm (24in) into the ground so it doesn't move. Insert the stake on the side of the prevailing wind so the tree isn't blown into the stake.

Preventing animal damage

Depending on where you live and how rural your garden is, you may need to provide protection from animals. Deer and grey squirrels can damage the bark on a new tree, killing it. Rabbits can also eat the bark on young trees, causing problems. Other mammals, such as voles, can nibble at a tree but are unlikely to cause major problems. Using mammal-proof tree guards can prevent the worst damage.

Planting into a pot

Some trees, such as dwarf apples, Japanese maples and olives, can grow quite well in pots. Choose the largest pot you have room for and use a peat-free, loam-based compost such as John Innes No. 3. Add compost to about one-third of the pot's depth. Place the tree in the pot on the compost to check how it will sit – it needs to be at the same level as it was growing in the ground. When you're happy with the depth, back-fill with compost and water thoroughly. See p.153 for care of a tree in a pot.

Planting a hedge

Hedges can be planted in single or double rows, depending on how big a space you have and how dense you want the hedge to be.

After planting

You may consider adding an organic mulch around the tree after planting and watering. Use garden compost, composted bark or wood chips, or well-rotted animal manure. Simply apply a thick layer around the base of the tree, but not against the trunk. Not only will this preserve water and suppress weeds, it will also slowly feed your newly planted tree, as well as feeding soil microbes such as bacteria and fungi, which in turn aid tree growth. Water the tree well, then keep it watered during dry spells for at least the first year.

Choosing a fruit tree

Fruit trees are available in many shapes and sizes so it's possible to choose one to suit the space you have, from a large spreading tree to one that grows against a fence, or one that thrives in a pot. The size is controlled by the rootstock that the tree is growing on, while the shape can be determined by pruning. A little research before you buy will help you to choose the most suitable tree.

Fruit trees are sold at different ages and sizes, depending on how they will be grown. A "whip" is up to one year old and about 1m (3ft) tall, with a central stem and few or no branches. A "feathered whip" is older and up to 2m (6½ft) tall, with side branches. A "maiden" is similar to a whip but usually produced by budding or grafting (see Rootstocks). A feathered maiden is older, with six branches. A bush fruit tree is two to three years old and has been pruned to form a head of several main branches. If growing a fruit tree as a standard, then a two- to three-year-old bush tree, where the formative pruning has been already done for you, is ideal. For a trained tree (see opposite), go for a whip or a maiden, as they're easier to prune into the shape you want.

Rootstocks

Some trees are grafted onto the root system of another tree, known as a rootstock. This controls the growth and vigour of the tree, so that it grows smaller (or sometimes more strongly) than it would on its own roots. This is useful when training a tree into a particular shape where less vigorous growth is needed. A rootstock can also improve disease resistance and control when and how much a tree fruits. Some are best for trees in pots. Often used for fruit trees, rootstocks are also used for some ornamentals.

Rootstocks have names such as "dwarfing" and "semi-dwarfing" and a code (in Britain there are M or MM rootstocks). Other rootstocks include Quince, Gisela and Colt. One of the most popular is MM106 (semi-dwarfing), used for apple trees. Some guidance is given on rootstocks in the fruit tree profiles (see pp.64–77).

Pollination

Most fruit trees are pollinated by insects, such as bees. Some, including apples and pears, need a "pollination partner" for the most successful fruit development. A pollination partner is simply another tree of the same genus that flowers at the same time, to enable cross-pollination to occur. Check these needs when buying your fruit tree; a specialist nursery will be able to offer reliable advice.

Untrained fruit trees

A standard is a typical-shaped fruit tree with a bare trunk and branches and is over 2m (6½ft). A specimen up to 4m (13ft) tall gives instant impact, but will grow very slowly. A standard is best grown on M9 for a small apple, or MM111 or M25 for larger trees, Quince A for pears, Colt for a cherry or plum and St Julien A for a peach.

Trained fruit trees

Fan and espalier These attractive trees are trained flat into a fan shape or, for an espalier, with horizontal branches. Train them up a fence or wall or along wires to mark a boundary. Growing the tree against a vertical surface, with its branches exposed, allows the sun to reach and ripen the fruits more easily. A fan or espalier needs to be pruned annually (see pp.160–61). It is best grown on a dwarfing or semi-dwarfing rootstock such as MM106 or M9 for apples, the semi-vigorous St Julien A for plums, Gisela 5 and Colt for cherries, Quince A for pears, and Torinel for peaches.
Stepover tree This is the smallest fruit tree, and is low growing, ideal for edging borders and paths. It is best grown on M27 for apples, Pixy for plums and Quince C for pears.
Cordon tree This is a small tree usually planted in a row to make a fruiting hedge. It is grown on a single stem with short side branches and needs to be planted 0.75–1m (2½–3ft) from others in the row and tied to supporting wires. It is best grown on a dwarfing rootstock such as M9 for apples, Pixy for plums and Quince C for pears.

Supporting your trained tree

By training your tree you are committing to regularly pruning it to maintain its shape (see pp.160–61). Support is key, too: even those grown against a wall or fence will need tying into supports (such as wires or bamboo canes) for the first few years.

Caring for your tree

Ultimately, a tree doesn't need much care, but in the first couple of years you will need to keep a close eye out to ensure your garden tree is growing well. A pot-grown tree will need extra care in the form of watering, feeding and top-dressing — but all newly planted trees need watering when conditions are dry. Checking the stake every now and then is important, too.

Just like any plant you add to your garden, you want your tree to do well. So check on it regularly, assess what it needs, and then provide it. Your tree will grow beautifully.

Watering a tree in the ground

Mature trees have extensive root systems, aided by fungi, that enable them to draw up water from the soil. The root systems of most trees are as wide as their canopy, but some also have deep taproots that extend far below the soil's surface, where they can literally "tap" into a water source usually unavailable to other plants.

A newly planted tree won't have an established root system to rely on yet, so will need some help from you. It's a good idea to water your tree every few weeks for up to two years after planting. This will help it become established and develop a good root system. Don't overthink the process — water weekly in the first six months (more if you're on sandy soil or conditions are particularly dry and sunny), ensuring the soil around the tree is completely soaked with each application — use one to two whole watering cans of water. Reduce this to every couple of weeks to a month as the tree grows, and be mindful of the seasons — don't water at all in winter, and check before watering in early spring, when the soil is often cold and wet.

Bear in mind that it's possible to over-water your tree, which will then produce roots close to the surface of the soil, making it more vulnerable to drought and more likely to topple in high winds. Check the soil if you think you may be watering too much.

Using a trowel, dig down to a depth of 5cm (2in). If the soil is dry and dusty, water. If it's damp, hold off watering for another week.

Feeding

Most trees don't need regular feeding, but an annual mulch of well-rotted manure or garden compost provides a slow-release nutrient boost for your garden tree. For the best results, water before applying the mulch, as the mulch will then conserve moisture as well as feeding the soil.

Weeding

Keep an area 1m (3ft) in diameter around your tree free from weeds, as these can quickly grow and smother your tree, especially if it's a sapling, and compete with the tree for water and nutrients. Weeds such as bindweed can engulf a young tree, causing growth to become distorted. Some rootstocks (usually those for espalier, stepover and pot-grown fruit trees, such as M27 and M9 for apples, Quince C and Quince Eline for pears, Pixy for plums and Gisela for cherries) need weed- and grass-free soil to grow well. For these, you may need to ensure bare soil around your tree trunk for its whole life, or mulch regularly to suppress weed growth.

Checking the stake

Newly planted trees are staked to prevent "wind rock", where wind moves the tree from side to side, tearing new roots, and preventing the tree from establishing well. It can take two years for a tree to anchor itself into the soil. It's worth keeping an eye on your tree stake as it can become loose and stop supporting the tree. Also bear in mind that you will need to loosen your tree tie as the tree grows, to prevent rubbing injury to the trunk. If you're using a tree guard, check it to ensure it's not cutting into the tree or hasn't come loose, and dispose of it responsibly when it's no longer needed.

Caring for a tree in a pot

Some trees can grow well in pots, but bear in mind that their roots are exposed to a finite amount of soil, water and nutrients, along with fungi, bacteria and microbes that aid tree growth. This means you will have to water more often, even if it rains. To keep the soil fresh and replenish some nutrients, each spring scrape off the top layer of compost and replace with a top-dressing of fresh, loam-based compost. Add a fortnightly dose of liquid feed in spring and summer as well, especially for fruit trees.

Planting around your tree

You may be content with planting just the tree in your garden, leaving it as the main focal point and having nothing growing around it. That's fine, but as an alternative you can plant shrubs and herbaceous plants around the tree to create a beautiful border, which not only adds interest but also provides additional habitats for wildlife, absorbs more carbon and helps prevent flooding.

Two options for your tree are to make it part of a sunny or shady (woodland) border, where it will work with the shrubs and perennials to create a look and habitat that changes through the seasons. Choose carefully and the shrubs and perennials will flower and/or fruit at different times of year from the tree, creating a longer season of interest.

If your tree is deciduous, grow an evergreen shrub nearby that will draw attention in winter from the tree's bare branches to something more lush and "alive". If your tree flowers in spring, choose perennials that flower in summer. If your tree has bold autumn colours, choose plants with a plainer overall look at this time of year, that will act as the perfect foil for your end-of-season display – or complementary colours that will enhance the tree's autumn hues. Plants work together above and below ground, sharing nutrients and information, but with a little input from you, they can be put together to make something special. You can add bird and bee boxes to enhance the wildlife appeal (see p.162).

Bear in mind that your tree will absorb a fair amount of water and the soil will therefore be drier here than in other parts of the garden. Also the tree's canopy will cast some shade beneath it. Even in a sunny border you will need some shade-tolerant plants, and plants that can cope with drier than average soil conditions.

Plants for a woodland border

A cool, shady area makes the perfect spot for a woodland border. Trees that would work in a woodland border include birch (see pp.108–09), hawthorn (see pp.84–85), Japanese maple (see pp.126–27), snowy mespilus (see p.55), tree ferns (see p.59) and dogwoods (see pp.90–91).

Under these you can plant shade-tolerant shrubs such as guelder rose (*Viburnum opulus*), spindle (see p.101) and holly (see pp.80–81), and herbaceous plants such as Solomon's seal (*Polygonatum × hybridum*), false goats' beard (*Astilbe*), campions (*Silene*), foxgloves (*Digitalis*), ferns and hostas, and low perennials such as hellebores, primroses (*Primula*), wood anemones (*Anemone nemorosa*) and sweet woodruff (*Galium odoratum*). In spring, add bulbous plants such as snowflakes (*Leucojum*) and snake's head fritillary (*Fritillaria meleagris*), while autumn-flowering Japanese anemones (*Anemone hupehensis*) will tolerate dappled shade.

Plants for a sunny border

There's a huge range of plants for growing in sun and dappled shade. Trees for a sunny border are crab apple (see pp.56–57), most fruit trees, olive (see pp.60–61), strawberry tree (see pp.98–99), crape myrtle (see p.87) and paperbark maple (see p.135). For a more exotic look, a palm could be an option here, too (see pp.136–43).

Shrubs include buddleia, weigela and rock rose (*Cistus*), while herbaceous plants include catmint (*Nepeta*), lavender (*Lavandula*) and other Mediterranean herbs, ornamental poppies (*Papaver*), agapanthus, bellflowers (*Campanula*) and annuals such as sunflowers (*Helianthus*).

Add vibrant colours against a lush green backdrop and you won't go far wrong. Plan to have something in flower from spring to autumn for a lively display and the most wildlife value. Add ornamental grasses such as *Stipa* and *Miscanthus* for structure and a longer season of interest. The best spring bulbs for bees are crocus and alliums, while viper's bugloss (*Echium*) attracts a wide range of pollinators. *Verbena bonariensis*, heleniums and rudbeckias will provide a late source of nectar and pollen.

How to plant your border

It can be difficult to get plants to establish immediately around trees, as light and soil moisture levels will be lower, but planting 1–2m (3–6½ft) from the trunk should be fine. Plants usually establish better on the sunny side of a tree's trunk. Plant in autumn for the best results, paying attention to planting depths and aspect requirements on the plants' labels.

Pruning
your tree

Many trees need some pruning at some stage of their life, but you may be surprised to learn that, with the exception of fruit trees, most can be left alone, with minimal pruning. However, a quick prune once a year can keep your tree healthy and maintain a good shape. This can be a good opportunity to check your tree for signs of pests and disease, which can prevent problems in the long term.

Most routine pruning involves using techniques to limit the size of the tree, improve its shape or, in the case of fruit trees, encourage more flowering (and therefore fruiting) spurs to form (see pp.160–61). Pruning to remove crossing, dead or damaged stems is also worthwhile, and can prolong the health of your tree. In some (thankfully rare) cases, you may need to prune out infection, such as canker (see p.166) or silver leaf disease (see p.167).

When to prune
Deciduous trees are usually pruned in winter, as it's easier to see what you're doing to the branches and to assess the overall shape. Exceptions include tender deciduous trees, which are best pruned in late spring, and stone fruit trees (including cherries,

apricots, peaches, plums and nectarines), which are best pruned in summer to prevent infection from the diseases silver leaf and bacterial canker. Some trees, such as walnut (*Juglans regia*) and mulberry (see p.77), bleed heavily (ooze sap from the pruning wound), so need to be pruned at certain times of year to avoid long-term damage.

While less likely to need pruning, evergreen trees should be pruned in spring, before growth starts, apart from pine trees, which need to be pruned in summer.

Preparing to prune
Before pruning, make sure you check if the tree has a Tree Preservation Order (TPO) in place or if the tree is in a Conservation Area – even newly planted trees are protected

PLANT, PRUNE, CARE

in conservation areas. You may need permission from the council first.

For safety, always check the tree before starting – especially older trees. Thick gloves, goggles and a hard hat are necessary for working on mature trees, when branches could fall on you or you could get sawdust in your eyes. Young trees have fewer, if any, such risks. If you're in any doubt, employ a professional tree surgeon to do the work for you.

Always use the sharpest secateurs, loppers and pruning saw, as these will ensure the cleanest cuts. If handling diseased material, clean your tools with antibacterial and anti-fungal solution to prevent spreading the infection to other parts of the tree.

Pruning a deciduous tree

When you plant a tree you may need to carry out some formative pruning to encourage the development of a good initial shape. Many nursery-grown trees will already have had some formative pruning, which you'll simply need to keep up.

However, if you grow a tree from a very young whip you'll need to prune it yourself to help the tree develop a good shape, with a clear trunk, and well-branched canopy. Remove sideshoots from the bottom third of

---

How to make a pruning cut

Make each cut carefully to reduce the risk of infection and keep the tree growing into a shape you want.

Cutting to a bud
Make a clean cut just above a bud. Angle the cut away from the bud so moisture doesn't pool on the wound. Don't leave too much stem above the bud as this will die back, attracting disease.

Cutting back to the stem or trunk
When removing a young shoot, cut it back flush with the stem using a clean cut so that the bark heals well.

---

the tree to ensure a strong, central trunk, then cut by half all of the sideshoots in the middle of the stem. Leave those at the top unpruned to form the initial branch framework.

For the basic methods and principles of regular pruning, see opposite. For detailed advice on pruning specific trees, consult a tree pruning book or visit rhs.co.uk/advice/plant-care/pruning.

Pruning a mature tree

You may inherit an old tree that needs a prune to reshape it or reduce its size. This is usually done to thin the canopy to allow in sunlight (especially for fruit trees), to raise the canopy to enable people or cars to move beneath it, or to reduce the tree's height. Bear in mind that bad pruning can make a mature tree unstable or look unsightly, and you may be best off getting in the professionals.

Pruning an evergreen tree

Evergreens only need minimal pruning: removing dead, diseased or broken branches, taking care to follow the general shape of the tree. Prune just before new growth starts in spring, using secateurs to tackle one branch at a time. The exception to this rule is pine trees, which should be pruned during active growth so new buds will develop in time for the following year.

Shears can be used for some trees but this creates a uniform, formal look that's best for evergreens. If creating a formal shape with shears, wait until late spring so growth has started, which will help cuts heal quickly. Most conifer trees grow on new wood only, so should be pruned back to new (pliable) growth. Pruning back into old, brown wood will result in unsightly brown patches that never grow back.

Pruning a palm

Palm trees are fairly low maintenance and don't need pruning, but you might want to tidy up brown fronds from time to time. Do this from late spring to summer, removing hanging, dead or otherwise unhealthy looking fronds. Avoid removing green fronds, especially new ones, as this can stress the tree.

Pruning a hedge

Hedges will need a regular trim, up to twice a year for formal hedges but ideally every other year for wildlife hedges, to avoid pruning out the eggs of some moth species. Remember that it's illegal to disturb bird nests

General pruning

While most ornamental trees need very little pruning, some (especially fruit trees) may need pruning annually to keep them in good shape. Before starting, work out what you want to achieve. Aim for an open shape so that light and air can reach all the branches.

Damaged branch
Remove any damaged branches, cutting just above the branch collar – the swollen area at the base of the branch, from where a scar can form more easily, aiding healing.

Diseased branch
Cut diseased branches to the trunk, again making sure that you don't cut into the branch collar. Check that you are cutting back to healthy wood.

Crossing branches
Remove any branches that are crossing and could rub together, causing wounds, which can weaken the tree, making it more susceptible to diseases.

Removing suckers
Pull suckers from the tree base by hand, or cut them to the ground with secateurs. Suckers from a grafted rootstock may be a different species to your tree.

so you must check your hedge thoroughly before trimming.

For yew hedges, initially shorten side branches only, to encourage a more dense growth habit. Wait until the hedge has reached the desired height before cutting the growing tips, as trimming the growing tips can pause growth for a year or two, making it very slow to establish.

Pruning a freestanding fruit tree

Fruit trees should ideally be pruned each year to keep them healthy and producing a larger crop. Unpruned fruit trees grow less productive over time, and can become congested.

Apple and pear trees Prune freestanding apples and pears when they're dormant in winter, after the leaves have fallen and before the buds burst. Aim to create an open, goblet or bowl shape with four to five main branches. Shorten the previous season's growth by a third, cutting back to an outward-facing bud so the tree retains an open form. Apples and pears are pruned according to where

Identifying fruiting buds

Like ornamental trees, fruit trees need to be pruned to remove dead, diseased or crossing branches. But they should also be pruned to maximise productivity. Learn to identify fruiting buds so that you can tailor your pruning to the type of tree you have.

Spur bearers bear fruit buds on wood older than two years, and as spurs, which can be identified as knobbly buds growing more closely together than the smaller leaf buds.

Tip bearers have their fruit buds at the tips of one-year-old shoots. They have a more untidy appearance than spur bearers. Partial tip bearers fruit on the tips and some spurs.

PLANT, PRUNE, CARE

their fruit buds form; as their name suggests, these are the buds that will form blossom and then fruits. Fruit trees are separated into three types: spur-bearers, partial tip-bearers and tip-bearers (see Identifying fruiting buds, opposite). Most apple and pear cultivars bought today are spur bearing, but if you're aware of how your tree fruits so you can prune it to maximise fruiting potential.

On spur-bearers, make sure that fruiting spurs are evenly spaced. If they are congested, thin them to 10–15cm (4–6in) apart. The result will be a balanced tree with plenty of light to ripen the fruits and space for air to circulate, discouraging disease.

On tip-bearers and partial tip-bearers, be aware that any pruning that involves shortening shoot tips will reduce the yield. Leave branches less than around 20cm (8in) long, and shorten longer ones to around four or five buds – as well as bearing fruit from those four or five buds, these cut stems will develop new shoots that will bear fruit the following year.

Plums and cherries Free-standing plums and cherries don't require as much pruning as apples and pears, but still benefit from formative pruning and then the thinning of old wood. Plums and other stone fruits such as cherries and apricots are pruned in early spring or midsummer to avoid infection by silver leaf disease.

Trees less than three years old should be pruned in late spring when the buds are bursting or when the tree is just beginning to flower. Shorten stems by around a third and remove damaged, diseased and crossing branches, aiming for an open goblet shape to maximise airflow and ensure the sun reaches the fruit.

Pruning a trained fruit tree

Fruit trees grown as espaliers, fans and cordons need to be pruned in summer and winter to maintain a good shape and keep them fruiting well. Summer pruning from August usually involves removing new growth beyond the ripening fruit. Exact pruning techniques and timings differ, depending on the age of your tree. For example young trees (up to three years old) often need specific formative pruning to ensure they grow well.

Always check the RHS pruning advice before carrying out any pruning work on trained fruit trees to ensure you're working at the right time of year for the type of tree you're pruning, and that you're pruning out the correct material.

Making the most of trees

Whether it's the tree in your garden or trees in the local community, you can make the most of them in ways that bring benefits to the local community and wildlife, and to you and others. Once you've planted your tree, you might notice and get to know other trees in your area. If you're involved in community groups, there will be a whole network of trees out there to explore.

Activities centred around your tree can range from simply feeding the birds to nature walks and organised annual events.

Attracting more birds

Hang feeders from strong branches, fixing a tray beneath the feeder so seed doesn't spill onto the ground (which can attract rats). Choose high-quality seed mixes and straight seeds such as sunflower seed, with suet and peanuts added to the mix in winter. Clean the feeder regularly to prevent birds spreading diseases and refill it when needed – never let the food go mouldy.

Local trees can also be used to hang bird feeders. Check with your local council or community group to ensure that this is agreeable. If you're hanging a feeder on a community tree, you may be able to ask others to chip in with the cost of bird seed and maintenance.

Nest boxes can be used to provide homes for birds before the tree develops natural nesting holes. Don't nail the box to the tree but use wire to fix it around the trunk instead – check the wire annually to make sure it's not cutting into the tree bark.

Making leaf mould

In nature, leaves fall to the ground and break down, gradually returning nutrients to the tree. By gathering leaves, rotting them down and then using them as a mulch in the form of leaf mould, you can mimic this natural process. Leaf mould is a fantastic resource. Essentially decomposed leaf material, aided by fungi rather than bacteria (as in conventional composting), it contains soil conditioners and trace elements that help your garden grow better. It has many uses – for example, as a mulch around the garden and allotment, and as an ingredient in home-made potting compost.

To get the best results, you simply pile leaves together, either in a bespoke bin or cage, or in a plastic bag with a few small holes for ventilation (old compost bags work well) for between one and three years. Then distribute the resulting leaf mould around the garden.

The leaves of all deciduous trees make good leaf mould, but break down at different rates. Thin, matt leaves such as birch, hazel, ash and elm, break down in less than 12 months, while waxy leaves such as oak and plane take up to three years. Evergreen leaves and conifer needles take much longer and benefit from being chopped up first.

If you're a member of your local "Friends of" park group, you can suggest leaf-gathering days where leaves from park trees are raked up and stored. Keep them for one year to use as a mulch around the park, or up to three to use in potting mixes.

Community activities

Use your community trees as part of a local nature trail, with signs in and around the trees to identify birds and other wildlife that might visit them. You may be able to get permission to let grass grow long around the trees, creating small pockets of meadow to enhance biodiversity. You could organise tree-centred Easter egg hunts and ID and drawing events for children. If there is a local mini-orchard you could have harvesting and pruning days. Take your neighbours out on bird and bat walks – you'll be amazed how much local wildlife uses the trees you planted.

Resources

For help identifying local trees and engaging with your community of trees, download a tree ID app on your phone or buy a simple tree book (you may find the tree ID guide listed on p.169 helpful). Once you've learned your trees, then focus on the birds and other species that use them. There's a whole world out there to explore and get to know – start in your garden or local park and you never know where your new knowledge might take you.

Troubleshooting

Pests and diseases are a common problem for growers of fruit trees and some deciduous trees, with climate change bringing new challenges. Both pests and diseases are a part of life, and many trees can live with them (although perhaps not with as much vigour as they would otherwise). But in both cases, you may sometimes have to help your tree to deal with a problem.

In this section I will mention some pests and diseases that are particularly widespread or harmful, so that you can recognise them if they affect your tree.

Pests and diseases in the garden

In gardening circles, "pest" is used to describe anything from slugs and snails to sawfly, aphids, ants and thrips, moth caterpillars and leaf-mining fly larvae that are perceived to damage plants. Most of these are not only part of the ecosystem but part of the food chain, and are essential for the survival of other species such as birds. With the exception of slugs and snails, the "damage" caused by them is usually minimal – there's no need to control them on garden trees. However, sometimes, and usually when growing in a compromised ecosystem with few predators such as birds and wasps, these "pests" can multiply faster than usual. A pest, in my view, is only such when present in sufficient numbers to do actual harm. As an apple grower I know some of my fruit will have codling moth tunnels in them, and so I cut my apples before I eat them, and eat around the tunnels. That's how I manage the "pest".

That said, there's an increasing number of non-native insects that have found their way to the British Isles and have no natural predators to keep their numbers in check. A few arrived of their own accord but most were accidentally imported on timber or live plants from other countries. Species from warmer climates can't usually survive our winters, but with climate change, some are managing to and more will do so in future.

Mammals and birds are also sometimes regarded as pests. Deer, squirrels and rabbits can damage bark, which can kill young trees These are best dealt with by using a tree guard (see p.149). Birds are considered pests for eating fruit crops such as cherries. Some gardeners net their cherry trees, but I'd rather share my crop with them – there's usually enough for us all.

Many trees can live with a level of infections. However, several new diseases have arrived in recent years, again usually due to importing plants and timber, which are having devastating consequences. There are many more diseases which could hit our shores in the coming years, and which experts are keeping an eye on. In the following pages, I've described some of the more common pests and diseases, grouped by the part of the tree most likely to be affected.

Pests and diseases that affect leaves and twigs

Aphids There are many species of aphid, which suck sap from trees and other plants. Most do little harm to the tree, and are eaten by a number of birds, including house sparrows.

Tree aphids suck plant sap and excrete a sugary substance called honeydew. Honeydew can attract black mould, which coats the leaves and can inhibit photosynthesis, weakening the tree. Woolly aphids are noticeable as they hide in white, waxy fluff. They're found on ornamental apple trees, cotoneaster and pyracantha shrubs. Affected stems sometimes develop swellings along the bark, which can burst in winter, creating wounds that expose the tree to fungal infections.

Box moth (*Cydalima perspectalis*) Native to East Asia, box moth was first found in Britain in 2007 (its caterpillars in 2011). The caterpillars eat box and cause severe defoliation. This pest is why you won't find box listed in the tree profile pages.

Horse chestnut leaf miner (*Cameraria ohridella*) This moth is native to Southern Europe and lays eggs on horse chestnut leaves. The larvae bore into the leaves, causing them to drop. In large numbers, and over several years, they can weaken trees, but there's some evidence that blue tits are starting to eat them.

Oak processionary moth (*Thaumetopoea processionea*) Native to southern Europe, oak processionary moth feeds exclusively on oak trees. Caterpillars form large, arrow-shaped groups on oak tree trunks, and can sometimes be seen moving between oak trees. They form large nests on oak trunks and large branches. The caterpillars are covered in small white hairs which can cause breathing difficulties in humans. If you do find this moth in your garden or elsewhere, submit a Tree Alert via forestresearch.gov.uk.

Canker (*Pseudomonas syringae*) Bacterial canker is a common disease of the stems and leaves of *Prunus*, especially plums and cherries, but also apricots and peaches. It causes sunken patches of dead bark, which oozes gum, and small holes in leaves, called "shothole". Trees can live with canker for years without dying, but severe cases can kill the tree. Using the cleanest and sharpest tools, you can literally cut the canker out of the branch. Prune back to around 10-15cm (4–6in) from the affected area, into healthy wood. Clean tools using disinfectant afterwards, to avoid spreading the infection.

Pests and diseases that affect fruits

Apple codling moth (*Cydia pomonella*) This small moth has caterpillars which bore into apples and pears in summer. The exit hole is usually visible, but the damage is most obvious when the fruit is cut open, and you can see the the tunnel.

Brown rot (*Monilinia laxa, M. fructigena*) This fungal disease affects apples, pears, plums, cherries and some ornamental trees, causing brown, rotting patches on the fruit. As the fruits ripen, they develop rotting brown patches, often with white pustules. The best way to control the fungus is to stop it overwintering. Remove all infected fruit in autumn, and either put it in your council green bin or bury it more than 1m (3ft) below ground.

Diseases that affect the whole tree

Honey fungus (*Armillaria* spp.) This attacks and kills the roots of woody and perennial plants, including trees. It's fairly common and is the worst fungal disease in gardens although some species are less aggressive than others and may not kill their host. The most obvious symptom is white fungal growth between the bark and wood, while clumps of light brown toadstools may appear in autumn. Black, shoe-lace-like strands called rhizomorphs may be found in the trunks of felled trees.

It's not possible to control honey fungus; the only way to get rid of it is to dig up and destroy affected plants, with as much of the root as possible.

Silver leaf (*Chondrostereum purpureum*) Silver leaf is a fungal disease that affects the wood and leaves of some trees, notably apples, apricots, cherries, plums, hawthorn, poplar and laburnum. The fungus usually penetrates the wood through pruning wounds. Leaves develop a silvery sheen before the whole branch dies. Older, dead branches may display bracket-shaped fruiting bodies in summer, whiteish on top and purple-brown below. When cut, the wood is stained. Infectious spores are most prevalent in winter, so susceptible trees should be pruned in summer. To control silver leaf, remove the affected branch as soon as possible, cutting it back to 10–15cm (4–6in) beyond any stained internal wood. Disinfect all tools afterwards and burn or dispose of the infected wood, as it can still fruit when cut and release spores that can reinfect your tree. Don't confuse silver leaf with false silver leaf, which causes silvery leaves, usually due to cold, drought or other stress. Unlike true silver leaf, which affects one branch at a time, the whole tree is affected and the wood is not stained.

Dutch elm disease (*Ophiostoma ulmi*) This fungal disease was accidentally brought from Canada in the 1960s and is spread by elm bark beetles. Some 60 million elm trees have been lost to the disease in Britain, and management continues to stop it taking out remaining stock.

Ash dieback (*Hymenoscyphus fraxineus*) Accidentally imported from Europe in 2012, but originating in Asia, ash dieback infects trees via airborne spores that penetrate the tree's leaves, and then grow inside the tree. Eventually, it blocks the xylem tissues, which transport water around the tree, resulting in its death. There is no remedy. According to the Woodland Trust, it could wipe out 80 per cent of our ash trees.

Fusarium wilt (*Fusarium oxysporum*) This fungal disease affects palm trees, including Canary Island date palm. Symptoms include browning of the fronds and dieback of the frond tips, starting at the base of the plant. Palms can be infected for years before symptoms develop, but the tree usually dies. Like other wilt diseases, including Verticillium wilt, Fusarium is soil borne and is often spread in nurseries. It can also be spread by pruning, so sterilise pruning tools after each use.

Supporting tree-planting projects

Beyond your community, you may want to support tree-planting projects to help get more trees in the ground. Bear in mind, however, that tree planting projects can be hugely problematic, so do your research. Here, I cover some of the pitfalls and recommend a few valuable organisations.

Some organisations are better than others – for example, you may not realise you're donating money to plant trees on rented land, with nothing to guarantee the trees will remain after the land's lease is up. Or, in some countries, that the trees are to be planted on land important to indigenous communities, many of which were not considered or consulted. The Great Green Wall project (see p.24) is only now involving local communities, some 15 years after its inception and after millions of the planted trees died.

And will you ever know if the trees you fund are planted in a way that contributes to the local environment, or if lots of the same tree are planted in straight rows, which have little if any options for wildlife? And will they be cared for so that they absorb carbon dixoide, or left to die so they release it back into the atmosphere?

TREES FOR LIFE

treesforlife.org.uk
My favourite tree planting scheme is based in Scotland, where just 2 per cent of the original Caledonian Forest remains. Here, through a combination of rewilding and planting native saplings grown from local seed, Trees for Life is reforesting the gaps between existing patches of woodland.

TREES FOR CITIES

treesforcities.org
Trees for Cities works with volunteers, schools and local communities in the UK and abroad, and has planted more than I million trees since 1993. It specialises in socially deprived urban areas.

THE WOODLAND TRUST

woodlandtrust.org.uk
Our largest woodland conservation charity, it buys up and saves threatened woods and plants new woodland (nearly 50 million trees since the 1970s).

Resources

RHS PRUNING INFORMATION

rhs.org.uk/pruning
Information on pruning a range of trees and tree types, with tips on time of year, hygiene and maximising fruiting potential.

GARDENERS' WORLD MAGAZINE

gardenersworld.com
Help and advice on growing and caring for trees and garden plants.

THE HIDDEN LIFE OF TREES

Peter Wohlleben, HarperCollins, 2015
How trees communicate, including the importance of fungal networks.

THE OVERSTORY

Richard Powers, Vintage, 2018
A fantastic novel about nine Americans who come together to address the destruction of the forests.

WHAT'S THAT TREE?

DK, 2013
Simple tree identification handbook.

WOODLANDS

Oliver Rackham, HarperCollins, 2012
One of the most significant voices on trees and woodlands in recent history, Oliver Rackham here documents the significance of trees and woodlands over time.

FRIENDS OF THE EARTH INTERNATIONAL FOREST PROGRAMME

foe.org/issues/forests/
How Friends of the Earth works to address the root causes of forest destruction and the marginalization of forest-dwelling communities.

GREENPEACE: PROTECT OUR FORESTS

greenpeace.org.uk/wp-content/uploads/2020/07/ GP-11-14-Forests-Final.pdf
Information on protecting forests from international environment trust dedicated to the conservation of forests and other ecosystems.

INTERNATIONAL TREE FOUNDATION

internationaltreefoundation.org
International charity for tree planting and conservation across the globe.

RAINFOREST ALLIANCE

rainforest-alliance.org
Charity dedicated to protecting rainforests across the globe.

REWILDING BRITAIN

rewildingbritain.org.uk
How rewilding can protect and restore UK habitats.

SOURCES FOR INFORMATION

p.6 In 2021, more than 400 weather stations broke their heat records:
www.theguardian.com/world/2022/jan/07/heat-records-broken-all-around-the-world-in-2021-says-climatologist

p.6 The Amazon rainforest is thought to emit more carbon dioxide than it can absorb:
www.sciencefocus.com/news/the-amazon-rainforest-now-emits-more-carbon-than-it-absorbs/

p.25 Half of Britain's new forests have been planted not by humans, but by jays:
www.theguardian.com/environment/2021/jun/16/half-the-trees-in-two-new-english-woodlands-planted-by-jays-study-finds

p.26 More than 50 per cent of people live in cities now, with nearly 70 per cent of the world's human population expected to live in cities by 2050:
www.un.org/development/desa/en/news/population/2018-revision-of-world-urbanization-prospects.html

p.26 A 2019 study predicts a 2°C (4°F) global rise by 2050 will see city temperatures rise exponentially higher:
www.bbc.co.uk/news/newsbeat-48947573

p.29 Some studies have also shown that street trees absorb less carbon dioxide than those growing in more natural environments:
www.frontiersin.org/articles/10.3389/fevo.2016.00053/full

p.50 One in eight homes don't have gardens:
www.ons.gov.uk/economy/environmentalaccounts/articles/oneineightbritishhouseholdshasnogarden/2020-05-14

Glossary

BLEEDING
The oozing of sap from a pruning cut after pruning.

BRACT
A modified, often flower-like leaf, usually growing around the flower.

BRANCH
A large, mature, woody stem.

BUD
A leaf or flower that has not yet opened.

CANOPY
The branches and foliage of a tree.

CARR
A wet woodland where trees adapted to wet soils, such as silver birch and alder, grow.

CATKIN
An elongated cluster of flowers, resembling a lamb's tail, with scaly bracts and typically no petals.

CONE
Usually found on pine trees, botanically it is a mass of scales or bracts, and contains the reproductive organs.

DETRITIVORE
Invertebrate such as an earthworm, that eats and recycles soil detritus.

DORMANCY/DORMANT
A stage of non-growth, typically in winter but occasionally in high summer.

DOUBLE FLOWER
A flower bred to have extra petals, often so many that you can't see the central part of the flower, where pollen and nectar is formed.

DRUPE
A fleshy fruit containing a single seed, such as cherry, peach or olive.

FLORET
A small flower, usually making up part of a head of flowers.

FRUITING SPUR
The fruiting buds of a tree, borne on small stems of wood.

HESPERIDIUM
A fruit with sections of pulp inside a rind, such as an orange or lemon.

INFLORESCENCE
A cluster of flowers.

LANCEOLATE
Used to describe leaves, shaped like a lance, tapering from a rounded base.

LEADER
The central stem (or trunk) of a tree.

NODE
The point on a stem from which a flower, leaf or twig will grow.

PALMATE
Used to describe leaves, shaped like a hand, having four or more lobes from a single point.

PANICLE
A multi-branched cluster of flowers.

PEDICEL
A small stalk, usually carrying a fruit.

PINNATE
Used to describe leaves, having a central stem with leaves growing on either side.

RIB
One of the main veins of a leaf.

ROOTSTOCK
The mass of roots some trees are grafted onto in order to control their size or protect from disease.

SAMARA
A winged fruit, carrying a seed or seeds.

SAPLING
A young tree, typically less than two years old.

SCALE
A small, thin, often dry structure, such as protective leaves around a bud or a piece shed from a leaf or bark.

SHOOT
Young, new growth (stem), often a fresher green than other stems.

SINGLE FLOWER
A flower where the central part containing the pollen and nectar are usually visible.

SPP.
Abbreviation for species (plural).

STANDARD
A tree grown in a uniform shape, with a single stem and distinct canopy.

STEM
Forming the skeleton of the plant, carrying nutrients between leaves and roots. In mature trees, this is the branches and twigs. Other stems, flowers, leaves and fruit grow from it.

SUCKER
New stem growing from the base of the tree, or rootstock.

TAPROOT
A long, single root growing deep into the ground.

TRUNK
The main woody stem of a tree, usually covered in bark, from which its branches grow.

TWIG
Small branch.

UMBEL
A flat cluster of flowers.

WHIP
A slender, unbranched shoot or plant, typically a tree seedling.

Planting zones

When researching trees to plant, you will see a hardiness rating for each. Below is a chart detailing temperatures and conditions for each hardiness rating, which will give you an idea of how well a tree will do in your garden. Only trees rated H2 and above are covered in this book.

RHS RATING	TEMPERATURE RANGE	CATEGORY	NOTES
H1a–c	Warmer than 15°C (59°F) to minimum 5°C (41°F)	Heated glasshouse required all year or for part of the year	A range from house plants to plants that can be grown outside in UK summer while temperatures are above minimum.
H2	1 to 5°C (34 to 41°F)	Tender – cool or frost-free glasshouse	Tolerant of low temperatures but will not survive being frozen. Can be grown outdoors once risk of frost is over.
H3	-5 to 1°C (23 to 34°F)	Half-hardy – unheated glasshouse / mild winter	Hardy in coastal/mild areas except in hard winters; at risk from sudden (early) frosts. Can survive with winter protection.
H4	-10 to -5°C (14 to 23°F)	Hardy – average winter	Hardy in most of the UK except inland valleys, at altitude and central/northerly locations. Plants in pots more vulnerable.
H5	-15 to -10°C (5 to 14°F)	Hardy – cold winter	Hardy through most of the UK even in severe winters. At risk in exposed sites, central/northerly locations, and in pots.
H6	-20 to -15°C (-4 to 5°F)	Hardy – very cold winter	Hardy throughout the UK and northern Europe. Many plants grown in containers will be damaged unless given protection.
H7	Colder than -20°C (-4°F)	Very hardy	Hardy in the severest European continental climates including exposed upland locations in the UK.

Index

Acknowledgments

Author acknowledgments
Thanks to the brilliant team at DK for coming up with the idea for this book and for asking me to write it. Special shout-outs to Amy Slack and Ruth O'Rourke for helping to put the book together and Jane Simmonds for painstakingly editing and cross-referencing it, including 50 tree profiles. Thanks also to Louise Brigenshaw and Mandy Earey for the design, and to Vivienne Watton for getting the book out there.

Thanks to my wonderful agent Jane Turnbull, who is always there with an ear and a solution to a problem. Thanks to Chris Young for overseeing the whole thing and for his never-ending positivity and cheerfulness. I really appreciate you letting me be honest about climate change and for giving me a platform to write about what I love the most on this wonderful Earth of ours: trees, plants and LIFE!

Thanks to Lucille Clerc for your amazing illustrations that transformed the book from a practical "how-to" to something you want to dive into and explore. Thanks to Kevin Martin, Head of the Arboretum at Kew, for your help on non-natives to grow in a changing climate, to Emma Crawforth at *BBC Gardeners' World Magazine* for always being on hand to answer random questions on tree IDs and varieties to grow. Thanks to Simon Maughan from the RHS for fact/sense-checking when I literally couldn't see the wood for the trees.

They were entirely useless in the creation of this book but I would like to thank Emma and Tosca for being my girls. Researching and writing about climate change isn't fun but they were always there to make me laugh. Tosca: stop growling at hedgehogs.

Illustrator acknowledgments
Thanks to the great team at DK and Kate Bradbury for their trust.

To my parents for teaching me to marvel at Nature everyday and to cultivate my own garden. Thanks to the wonderful man who taught me how to draw and to my ever-loving gardener mother, you two gave me inspiration for a lifetime.

To my partner for his daily support, may our love grow as strong as the Major Oak.

I wish all you readers the joy of planting a tree: to watch it grow and gather with your loved ones under its welcoming foliage, to share its fruits, and to pass it on to the next generation.

Publisher acknowledgments
DK would like to thank Francesco Piscitelli for proofreading and Vanessa Bird for indexing.

ABOUT THE AUTHOR

Kate Bradbury is an award-winning author and journalist, specialising in wildlife gardening. She edits the wildlife pages of *BBC Gardeners' World* magazine, and regularly writes articles for *The Telegraph*, *The Guardian*, *RHS The Garden* magazine, and *BBC Wildlife* and *Wildlife Trust* magazines. She is the author of several books, including *The Wildlife Gardener*, memoir *The Bumblebee Flies Anyway* (both Bloomsbury), and *RHS How to Create a Wildlife Pond* (DK). She lives in Brighton, where her small but perfectly formed garden is home to ALL the wildlife, including hedgehogs, frogs and toads, house sparrows, starlings and slow worms. She is ever hopeful of swifts. Her garden featured as part of the GardenWatch campaign for BBC *Springwatch* and *Autumnwatch*. Kate also appears on *BBC Gardeners' World*, where she demonstrates how to use garden plants to attract wildlife to small urban gardens, like hers. She's a patron of Froglife and Bumblebee Conservation Trust, and garden ambassador of Butterfly Conservation.

ABOUT THE ILLUSTRATOR

Lucille Clerc is a French graphic designer and illustrator based in London. She set up her studio after graduating from Central Saint Martins with an MA in Communication Design. She has illustrated a number of books and magazines, and has also created works for the fashion industry and exhibition spaces. Much of her work is inspired by London's architecture and the relationship between Nature and urbanisation, with her compositions portraying her favourite places and exploring their past and present lives.

DK UK
Project Editor Amy Slack
Senior Designer Louise Brigenshaw
Jacket Designer Amy Cox
Jackets Coordinator Jasmin Lennie
Production Editor David Almond
Production Controller Rebecca Parton
Ediorial Manager Ruth O'Rourke
Design Manager Marianne Markham
Art Director Maxine Pedliham
Publisher Katie Cowan

Illustrated by Lucille Clerc
Editor Jane Simmonds
Designer Mandy Earey
Consultant Gardening Publisher Chris Young

ROYAL HORTICULTURAL SOCIETY
Consultant Simon Maughan
Publisher Rae Spencer-Jones

First published in Great Britain in 2022 by
Dorling Kindersley Limited
DK, One Embassy Gardens, 8 Viaduct Gardens,
London, SW11 7BW

The authorised representative in the EEA is
Dorling Kindersley Verlag GmbH. Arnulfstr. 124,
80636 Munich, Germany

A Penguin Random House Company
001–321085–Sept/2022
10 9 8 7 6 5 4 3 2 1

A CIP catalogue record for this book is available from the British Library.
ISBN: 978-0-2414-5975-1

Printed and bound in China.

For the curious
www.dk.com

MIX
Paper from
responsible sources
FSC™ C018179

This book was made with Forest Stewardship Council ™ certified paper – one small step in DK's commitment to a sustainable future. For more information go to www.dk.com/our-green-pledge